Mastering LSAT Logic Games

Key Strategies for Setting up Logic Games and Solving the Questions

By Dr. Stephen Harris
Educational Testing Consultants, Inc.

ALL RIGHTS RESERVED. This book contains material protected under International and Federal Copyright Laws and Treaties. Any unauthorized reprint or use of this material is prohibited. No part of this book may be reproduced or transmitted in any form or by any means, electronic or mechanical, including photocopying, recording, or by any information storage and retrieval system without express written permission from the author / publisher.

LSAT is a registered trademark of the Law School Admission Council, which does not review or endorse specific test preparation materials or services. This work has not been reviewed or or endorsed by LSAC.

Published by Steve Schwartz
New York, New York

www.LSATUnplugged.com

Table of Contents

Foreword 3

Mastering LSAT Logic Games 5

   Introduction and Overview 5

      AR stimuli 7

      AR items 10

   Setting up Games 12

      Identify the type of game 12

      Choose a framework 13

      Write the rules 13

      Look for consequences of the rules 15

   Common logic game types 17

      Simple sequencing 18

      Sequencing with matching 20

      Simple grouping 23

      Common grouping notions, and their representations: 25

      Two groups with conditional rules 27

      Contrapositives 28

      Combining conditional rules 29

      Elements of different types 30

      Overlapping categories 33

      Sequencing groups of elements 34

      Multiple groups, (some) elements sequenced 36

      Sequencing categories/groups and elements 38

      Setting up games, conclusion 39

- Solving Items 40
  - The "could be true" family 42
  - Item solving strategies for the "could be true" family: example 44
  - The "must be true" family 54
  - Using possible arrangements of elements 62
- Rarer item types 69
  - Fixed elements/possible arrangements 69
  - Earliest/latest 71
  - Complete and accurate list 73
- Sample Games 76
- Conclusion 95

Foreword

Hey there,

I'm Steve Schwartz, founder of LSAT Unplugged (www.LSATUnplugged.com), a website devoted to sharing free and low-cost LSAT resources.

I got Dr. Stephen Harris, **a former writer of *actual* LSAT questions(!)** to write this book.

He was actually on the fence about it, but I knew just how valuable his knowledge was. So we talked, and talked, and talked some more, and finally he agreed to write this fantastic guide.

As you can imagine, having this experience has given him a tremendous amount of insight into solving the questions. He understands them in a way few other people do.

I can't overstate how great of a resource this is. This is like getting to talk to Michael Jordan about basketball, Meryl Streep about acting or Colonel Sanders about chicken.

This guide covers how to approach each major type of Logic Game and the questions associated with each one. It has several sections that really get into understanding the nuts and bolts of Logic Games and how they're built.

Thing is…this book only covers strategies for ONE section – it doesn't cover the other sections, and it doesn't give you explanations for the dozens of exams out there.

So, make sure you visit my website, LSAT Unplugged at www.LSATUnplugged.com, for tons of free LSAT resources, articles, guides, explanations, and more.

Here's what one student said:

"Your website was the best free resource I found online." - Max, 155 to 176

You can *also* join my free LSAT email course. I'll even give you my Easy LSAT Cheat Sheet as a free bonus.

See you on the other side,

Steve Schwartz

P.S. Feel free to email me at Steve@LSATUnplugged.com if you have any questions or need anything at all. I love hearing from students.

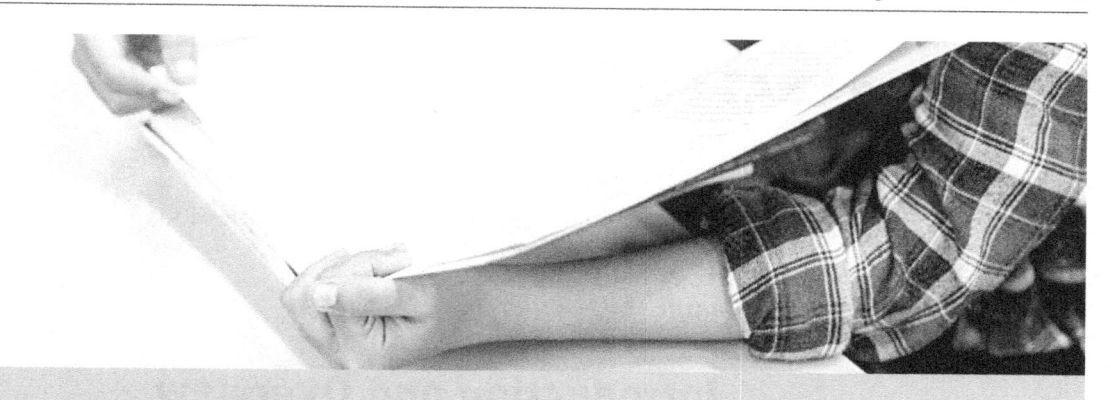

Mastering LSAT Logic Games

Key strategies for setting up logic games and solving the questions

Introduction and Overview

The analytical reasoning, or "logic games," section of the LSAT tests one's ability to recognize logical relations among objects, and to reason about them. This essentially involves drawing conclusions about how certain objects can be arranged from a set of rules governing their placement.

An analytical reasoning section has four separate logic games, and each game begins with a stimulus of two parts:

The first part, which we'll call the scenario, provides the real-world context for the logical relations to be discussed, as well as important information about the structure of the game.

The second part we'll call the rules. The rules dictate which arrangements of things introduced by scenario are allowable.

> Six diplomats – a foreign minister and a senior advisor from each of three countries, R, S, and T – travel by limousine from their hotel to a meeting. Six limousines numbered 1 through 6 arrive at the hotel, and exactly one diplomat enters each limousine. The limousines then depart for the meeting one at a time, in numerical order. The assignment of diplomats to limousines is governed by the following conditions: scenario

Key Strategies for Setting up Logic Games and Solving the Questions

> The diplomats in the first two limousines to depart are from the same country.
> The diplomat in limousine 3 is from a different country than the diplomat in limousine 4.
> Limousines 1 and 4 each carry either the foreign minister from R or the senior advisor from T.
> The senior advisor from S is not in the last limousine to depart.

⎫ rules

Each stimulus is followed by 5 to 7 items that are to be solved on the basis of that stimulus only.

Each item consists of an answer stem followed by five answer choices.
The items will ask about various features of the allowable arrangements of things, given the stimulus rules.

> Which one of the following pairs of limousines cannot give rides to diplomats from the same country? ⎫ stem
>
> (A) 3 and 5
> (B) 4 and 5
> (C) 3 and 6
> (D) 4 and 6
> (E) 5 and 6

⎫ answer choices

Recent AR sections have typically contained a total of 22-24 items. Thus, correctly answering 16 to 18 of the AR items on a test is consistent with a score in the high 150s to mid-160s on the LSAT as a whole.

7

AR stimuli

Although the real-world contexts for logic games vary tremendously from game to game, the logical structures underlying these games are very similar. This is because all logic games are constructed out of only two fundamental logical notions – ordering and grouping. The amazing variety of logic games found on the LSAT arises from the rich expressive capability of these two simple ideas, either alone or in combination

The logical notion most frequently employed in logic games is ordering, and in particular, sequencing. Fortunately, it is easy to spot ordering in a logic game – there will be clear indications of it, especially in the rules.

Ordering games are easy to set up since they usually involve placing things in a line, or sequencing things, as does this game:

> Seven job applicants—B, C, D, F, G, H, and J—are each scheduled for exactly one interview on the same day. The interviews are scheduled sequentially, one at a time. The order in which the interviews are scheduled is governed by the following conditions:
>
> C must be scheduled <u>before</u> H.
> J must be scheduled <u>immediately after</u> D.
> B cannot be scheduled <u>immediately before</u> or <u>immediately after</u> D.
> F must be scheduled <u>after</u> D and <u>before</u> C.
> G must be scheduled <u>immediately before</u> B.

Key Strategies for Setting up Logic Games and Solving the Questions

Grouping, the other key logical ingredient of logic games, is harder to spot, since common ways of expressing grouping are very context-dependent:

The Glass Slipper Shoe Shop has stores in exactly three locations: Waterside, Youngstown, and Zoobridge. Each store carries exactly two of the following five brands: Artistry, Bloom, Cerulea, Dash, and Forward Foot. Each of these brands is carried by at least one of the three stores. The brands are stocked according to the following conditions:

None of the stores carries both Artistry and Forward Foot. Waterside and Youngstown either both carry Cerulea, or neither of them does.

If Youngstown carries Bloom, then Waterside and Zoobridge both carry Dash.

Youngstown does not carry any brand that Zoobridge carries.

In this game the verb "to carry" indicates grouping – brands of shoes are grouped by store, depending on whether a store carries the brand. Groups can interact in complicated ways, making it much harder to determine how to set up grouping games. Often the most important step is choosing a diagram that allows one to represent these complicated interactions clearly.

Logic games often combine the two key notions, as does this game:

A four day music festival will feature six headlining bands—*Supa Menz, Tone Def, Vice Quad, Whine Iron, Youth Tunes*, and *Ziggurat*. Each band will play on exactly one day of the festival, and each day of the festival will feature at least one of the bands. The schedule of headlining bands must conform to the following conditions:

>No more than two of the bands will play on any day.
>*Vice Quad* will play on the day <u>immediately after</u> *Supa Menz*.
>Either *Supa Menz* or *Youth Sounds* will play on <u>the same day as</u> *Tone Def*.
>At most one of the bands will play on a day after *Whine Iron* plays.

In the present game, the order of bands is partially determined by which days they play on. But to the extent bands play on the same day, grouping is involved. So we'll have to attend to both features when setting up this game.

There are many ways that these notions can be utilized, both individually as well as in combination. But all this variety ultimately arises from just two basic logical building blocks – ordering and grouping.

AR items

AR items concern arrangements of elements based on the conditions specified by the stimulus. Most items (~90%) are members of one of only two item families – the "could be true" family, and the "must be true" family.

"could be true"

> If the minister from T rides in limousine 2, then which one of the following could ride in limousine 5?
>
> (A)   The advisor from R
> (B)   The advisor from S
> (C)   The advisor from T
> (D)   The minister from R
> (E)   The minister from S

This "could be true" item has two additional features that provide important clues as to how to solve it. First, it has a conditional stem, or stem in "if…then" form. Second, the stem is focused; that is, the stem describes specific features of the situation that serves as a solution to the item. Here we know that we are only concerned with determining who could ride in limousine 5.

"must be true"

Which one of the following must be true?

(A) The advisor from R rides in limousine 2.

(B) The advisor from S rides in limousine 3.

(C) The advisor from S rides in limousine 4.

(D) The minister from R rides in limousine 4.

(E) The minister from S rides in limousine 5.

By contrast, this "must be true" item has a categorical stem, and the stem is unfocused; it provides no additional description of the situation we are searching for. We'll return to the importance of these stem clues when discussing item solving strategies.

Just as logic games involve two separate families of skills — one for the stimuli and one for the items, mastery of the AR section generally proceeds through two stages:

- becoming familiar with the common ordering and grouping themes found in AR stimuli

- becoming familiar with the various items solving strategies and recognizing which strategies can be employed most efficiently on which items.

Test takers who reach the first stage find that they generally solve items correctly, but that they solve them more slowly than they would like. Still, one who reaches this plateau should be able to score 14 - 16 on the AR section, a score consistent with totals in the high 150s to low 160s. This requires only that one correctly complete two games, and then pick up a spare item or two on each of the remaining two games, including those items answered correctly as a result of random guessing.

Key Strategies for Setting up Logic Games and Solving the Questions

Test takers who reach the second stage and master the subtleties of strategy selection and implementation find that they have sufficient time to respond to most if not all of the items, and so should be able to regularly score in the 19 and above range on the AR section.

Setting up Games

Setting up logic games is a skill essential for success on the AR section. Game set-up requires one to:

- Identify the type of game
- Choose a framework
- Write the rules
- Look for consequences

Let's walk through the steps with the following stimulus:

Identify the type of game.

elements

Seven job applicants—<u>B, C, D, F, G, H, and J</u>—are each scheduled for exactly one interview on the same day. The interviews are scheduled sequentially, one at a time. The order in which the interviews are scheduled is governed by the following conditions:

C must be scheduled <u>before</u> H.

J must be scheduled <u>immediately after</u> D.

B cannot be scheduled immediately before or immediately after D.

F must be scheduled after D and before C.

G must be scheduled immediately before B.

The expressions "before," "immediately after," etc. in the rules of this game indicate that ordering is involved. Moreover, the scenario makes clear that things will be placed in a sequence.

We'll call the things that we sequence or group *elements*. In this game the elements are the letters at the top of the stimulus, as is common in sequencing games.

Choose a framework.

A convenient way to represent this type of game is to indicate positions in the sequence that the elements will occupy by means of small dashes. We'll place the elements onto these dashes to represent their relative order:

___ ___ ___ ___ ___ ___ ___

Write the rules.

A central theme to AR games is representing information in a way that makes it easy to grasp. The important point is that an insightful notation will allow one to represent facts spatially, which makes them easier to access and combine with other pieces of information from the game.

Key Strategies for Setting up Logic Games and Solving the Questions

In sequencing games this connection is clear and immediate; the rules typically place elements in relative order, so our notation should reflect these facts.

The following notation provides an efficient means to represent the kinds of facts typically found in ordering games.

"A is sometime before B"	A…B
"A is immediately before B"	A, B
"A is adjacent to B"	(A,B)
"A and B are not adjacent"	(A̶,B̶)

The use of ellipses and commas is clear enough.

We'll use parentheses to indicate that the relative order of elements is undetermined. For example, when we say that "A is adjacent to B" we know that the elements occupy spaces that are next to each other, but we do not know which element comes first, and so use parentheses to reflect this.

Additionally, we'll use a slash through an expression to represent "not."

In terms of this notation, then, the rules from the game above (also below) can be represented in the following way:

C must be scheduled before H.	C…H	(1)
J must be scheduled immediately after D.	D, J	(2)

B cannot be scheduled immediately before or immediately after D.	(B̶,̶ D̶)	(3)
F must be scheduled after D and before C.	D…F…C	(4)
G must be scheduled immediately before B.	G, B	(5)

Look for consequences of the rules.

Next comes the important step of combining the rules to yield new consequences. In sequencing games this often involves comparing rules that concern the same elements.

For instance, rules 2 and 4 both concern D. Since D and J are adjacent, this D-J pair must precede F and C, in that order; and by rule 1, H must be placed even further back, after C:

D, J…F…C…H

We now know the relative order of five out of seven elements. The only two elements not yet mentioned in our new "super-rule" are G and B.

By rule 5 G and B are adjacent, and in that order. But by rule 3, B and D cannot be adjacent, so the G-B pair cannot precede the D-J pair, and thus must follow it in the sequence, somewhere or other.

We'll let our rule branch to reflect the fact that the G-B pair must be placed after the D-J pair, but is otherwise independent of F, C, and H:

…G, B
D, J…F…C…H

The next step is to see which consequences can be represented directly in our diagram.

Since all five remaining elements must follow the D-J pair, these elements must occupy positions 1 and 2 in the sequence, respectively:

D   J

___ ___ ___ ___ ___ ___ ___

Moreover, only elements H and B have no elements behind them, so one or the other of these must be last in the sequence. Let's use a slash between elements to mean "or." We now have the following diagram and rules:

B C D F G H J

...G, B

D, J...F...C...H

D   J

___ ___ ___ ___ ___ ___ ___

                                                                       B/H

With so much information contained in our derived rule and diagram, we should be able to solve the items associated with this stimulus quickly and efficiently.

Common logic game types

Although logic games concern many different subjects and superficially bear very little resemblance to one another, all logic games are built out of one or another of two basic notions: ordering and grouping.

These two notions are amazingly versatile and richly expressive, and several distinct though related logical structures arise quite naturally from these building blocks. The following nine categories of games, each employing ordering or grouping in a characteristic way, provide a comprehensive survey of logic game types appearing on the LSAT.

Virtually every logic game appearing on the LSAT over the past 20 years is an instance of, or variation on, one of the following game types. Familiarity with the features of each of these game types is essential if you are to be well-prepared for the games that you will see on test day.

- Ordering Games

    Simple sequencing

    Sequencing with matching

- Grouping Games

    Simple grouping

    Two groups with conditional rules

    Elements of different types

    Overlapping categories

- Combination Games

    Sequencing groups of elements

    Multiple groups, (some) elements sequenced

    Sequencing categories/groups and elements

Key Strategies for Setting up Logic Games and Solving the Questions

Let's examine each of these game types in detail.

Simple sequencing

- Elements are named, but have no other distinguishing attributes

Example:

> A recent study rated six new car models-L, M, N, P, Q, and R-with respect to overall passenger safety. No two models received the same rating, and each of the six models received exactly one rating.
> The safety ratings assigned to the models by the study are consistent with the following conditions:
>
> Q received a higher safety rating than M.
>
> R received a safety rating one higher than P's safety rating.
>
> N received the fourth-highest safety rating.
>
> P received a higher safety rating than M.

The most common game type on the LSAT is the sequencing game. In the basic version the elements are named, but have no other distinguishing attributes. Standardly each element appears exactly once in the sequence, although a common variation is to allow repeated elements.

In this game six elements will be placed in a sequence based on relative safety rating as the presence in the rules of expressions such as "higher safety rating" and "lower safety rating" suggests. The diagram for this game can be six dashes in a line, as we've seen above.

The only additional catch here is deciding whether to order elements from highest safety rating to lowest, or *vice versa*. The expression "fourth-highest" suggests ordering from highest to lowest, but the best way to decide would be to see how elements are ordered in the answer choices of the items.

The rules can be represented easily enough, using the notation introduced above:

L M N P Q R

(1)   Q…M
(2)   R, P
(4)   P…M

___ ___ ___ _N_ ___ ___

Rules 2 and 4 combine in a familiar way – the R-P pair must precede M. And by rule 1, so must Q:

R, P…M

Q…

This next step is slightly trickier: notice that three elements must precede M in the sequence. But since N is in position 4, N must precede M as well; there's no room for M before N. But then the R-P pair must appear before N:

R, P…N…M

Q…

This leaves only two places to put the R-P pair – positions 1 and 2, or positions 2 and 3; either way, P or R is in 2.

Key Strategies for Setting up Logic Games and Solving the Questions

Moreover, L and M are the only elements that are not required to have elements behind them in the sequence, so either L or M must be last. Putting all the pieces together, we get the following set-up:

L M N P Q R

R, P...N...M

Q...

___ ___ ___ ___ ___ ___
      P/R   N   L/M

As this game illustrates, the key to sequencing games is attending to how far forward or backward in the sequence particular elements must be, and keeping in mind how the placement of a single element in the sequence affects the placement of the others, especially elements that must be adjacent to one another.

Sequencing with matching

- Elements are of two categories, usually one a property or attribute of the other
- Elements of one category are typically repeated

Example:

A museum's new exhibit will consist of exactly seven different paintings—G, H, J, K, L, M, and N. Each painting is placed along a gallery wall in positions numbered 1-7 from left to right. Some of the Paintings are by resident artists; the others are by visiting artists.
The following conditions must hold:
    G occupies the fourth position along the gallery wall.
    Both K and M are placed to the left of G on the gallery wall.

K is to the right of H on the gallery wall.

A painting by a visiting artist occupies the sixth position.

Each paining by a visiting artist is immediately preceded on the gallery wall by a painting by a resident artist.

N is a painting by a visiting artist.

Here the first category of elements is easy enough to spot – the letters corresponding to the paintings. But the second category is harder to spot – R and V.

Each position in the sequence is occupied by precisely one element of each type, as the stimulus makes clear. Not surprisingly, the rules will typically refer to positions using both categories of elements. The basic diagram remains the same; we just need to make space for two letters in each position. Additionally, it will make it easier to keep track of the different categories of elements if we use lower-case letters r and v in our diagram.

We'll represent the rules in the standard way, with a couple of twists. Rule 2 places both K and M to the left of G, but with their relative order undetermined; we'll use parentheses to represent this fact.

Rule 5, the second-to-last rule, is a bit tricky as well. Notice that this does not mean that rs and vs alternate. One way to represent this rule is simply to put a slash through "v, v." But one must not overlook that this rule requires position 1 to be an r, a fact we'll add directly to the diagram. Putting all these parts together, we get:

G H J K L M N

(2) (K...M)...G

(2) H...K

Key Strategies for Setting up Logic Games and Solving the Questions

```
                                              (5)  r̶,v̶
   r           G       v                      (6)  Nv
 ___  ___  ___ ___ ___ ___ ___
```

An important feature of this game, and matching games generally, is how the extra complexity of two categories of elements allows for rich consequences to be drawn from the rules.

To begin with, rules 2 and 3 place three elements in front of G – H, K, and M.

Since G is in position 4, these elements occupy all of the positions to the left of G, with either H or M in position 1, and K or M in position 3.

Thus the remaining elements all following G, in some order or another:

```
                                       H...K...G...(J...L...N)
                                       M...
                                                          y̶,v̶
   r           G       v                                  Nv
 ___  ___  ___ ___ ___ ___ ___
 H/M       K/M
```

Next, rule 5 requires that r's occupy positions 5 and 7. So N must occupy position 6, with J and L switching between positions 5 and 7:

```
                                       (K...M)...G...(J...L...N)
                                       H...K
                                                          y̶,v̶
   r           G   r   Nv  r                              Nv
 ___  ___  ___ ___ ___ ___ ___
 H/M       K/M   J/L     J/L
```

23

The time spent drawing these consequences will pay huge dividends once we turn to the items of this game.

Simple grouping

- Two categories of things – elements and group names

- Groups are independent

The Glass Slipper Shoe Shop has stores in exactly three locations: Waterside, Youngstown, and Zoobridge. Each store carries exactly two of the following five brands: Artistry, Bloom, Cerulea, Dash, and Forward Foot. Each of these brands is carried by at least one of the three stores. The brands are stocked according to the following conditions:
>None of the stores carries both Artistry and Forward Foot.
>Waterside and Youngstown either both carry Cerulea, or neither of them does.
>If Youngstown carries Bloom, then Waterside and Zoobridge both carry Dash.
>Youngstown does not carry any brand that Zoobridge carries.

Grouping games at first glance may resemble matching games, in that both types of stimuli typically introduce two categories of things. The easiest way to tell the difference is by checking the rules – this game's rules do not involve ordering, so it must be a grouping game! Since in grouping games more than one element from one category can be matched

Key Strategies for Setting up Logic Games and Solving the Questions

to each element of the other, it is natural to think of the one category as the group names for the collections of elements from the other. In this case, it makes sense to treat the locations W, Y, and Z as the groups, and the brands A, B, C, D, and F as the elements to be placed inside these groups. A simple grid is a handy diagram for these games, with group names along the top (order doesn't matter!) and elements placed into the corresponding columns in accordance with the rules:

```
  W  |  Y  |  Z
     |     |
     |     |
```

Grouping scenarios often contain crucial "ground rules" that govern the game set-up. Important things to check for include whether each element must occur at least once, whether elements can occur in more than one group, etc. The scenario of this game makes it clear that each element occurs at least once, that each group contains exactly two elements, and that elements may be repeated in different groups.

Writing the rules for grouping games typically involves keeping track of which elements must be in the same group as, or different groups from, each other. The following scheme for representing common grouping facts is helpful.

Common grouping notions, and their representations:

"A and B are in the same group" | a   b |

"A and B are in different groups" | a ╱ b |

"If A is in X then B is in Y"   Xa → Yb

"A is in every group B is in"   b → a

"Any element in X is in Y"   X → Y

An element is in X if and only if it is in Y"   X ↔ Y

Most grouping rules can be represented using the above notation, or obvious variations on it. An important difference between ordering games and grouping games is the frequency with which conditional relations, represented above by means of arrows, are expressed by the rules. We'll have occasion to examine these kinds of relations next, as we return to the rules of the present game:

> None of the stores carries both Artistry and Forward Foot.
> Waterside and Youngstown either both carry Cerulea, or neither of them does.
> If Youngstown carries Bloom, then Waterside and Zoobridge both carry Dash.
> Youngstown does not carry any brand that Zoobridge carries.

Key Strategies for Setting up Logic Games and Solving the Questions

Rules 1 and 3 can easily be handled using the notation above. Rule 2 is a bit tricky – If C is in both W and Y, or in neither W nor Y, then C is in W if and only if it is in Y. Finally, the conditional relation in rule 4 is not obvious: this rule amounts to saying that if an element is in Z then it isn't in Y. We'll use the tilde symbol for "not."

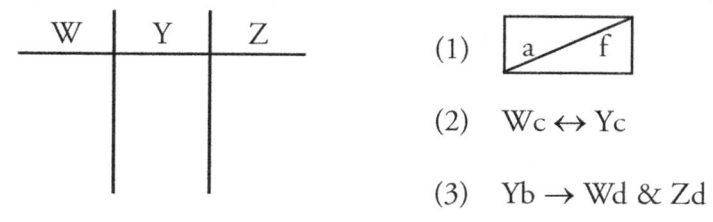

W	Y	Z

(1) [a / f]

(2) Wc ↔ Yc

(3) Yb → Wd & Zd

(4) Z → ~Y

Drawing consequences from the rules of grouping games is often a subtler process than it is with ordering games, and we'll develop the important themes as we work through various examples.

However, we'll make one observation now: there are five elements, but six possible positions, so exactly one element occurs twice. This observation allows one to conclude, for instance, that B and C cannot both be in Y, since by rule 2 C must then have two occurrences (X and Y), and by rule 3 D must then have two occurrences (W and Z).

We'll explore additional ways to draw consequences from grouping rules in the next game.

Mastering LSAT Logic Games

Two groups with conditional rules

- as above, with two groups and conditional statements for rules

A book club will select at least one of the following seven books: *House of Leaves, The Idiot, The Jungle, Lolita, Pale Fire, Slaughterhouse-five*, and *Ulysses*. The following restrictions on the selections must apply:

    If *Lolita* is selected, then either *Infinite jest* or *Slaughterhouse-five* is selected.

    If *Infinite Jest* is selected, then *House of Leaves* is also selected but *Pale Fire* is not.

    If *Slaughterhouse-five* is selected, then *Pale Fire* is selected but *Ulysses* is not.

    If *House of Leaves* is selected, then both *The Jungle* and *Ulysses* are also selected.

A very common type of grouping game is the two-group conditional rule game. At first this stimulus seems to run counter to the earlier observation, that grouping games involve two categories of things. But while the scenario mentions only that certain books will be selected, the rules make it clear that not being selected is also relevant to this game.

Thus, letters representing the books serve as the elements, while the groups are "selected" and "not-selected," which we'll represent as C and ~C (for "chosen" and "not chosen"). The rules of this game are all conditional statements, and have standard representations:

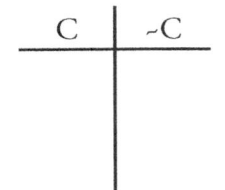

C	~C

(1)   L → I/S

(2)   I → H & ~P

(3)   S → P & ~U

(4)   H → J & U

Key Strategies for Setting up Logic Games and Solving the Questions

Contrapositives

Many test takers find it helpful to write the contrapositives of conditional rules. The contrapositive of a conditional statement is formed by switching the positions of, and negating, the component statements:

Conditional:	Contrapositive:
P → Q	~Q → ~P
P/R → Q	~Q → ~P & ~R
P & R → Q	~Q → ~P/~R

Notice that negating an "and" statement results in an "or" statement; and that negating an "or" statement results in an "and" statement. The contrapositive of a conditional statement is equivalent to the original conditional, but many people find it easier to recognize when a conditional rule applies if they write out both forms of the rule.

Returning to the present stimulus, then, here are the rules of the game, together with their contrapositives:

Rule:	Contrapositive:
L → I/S	~I & ~S → ~L
I → H & ~P	~H/P → ~I
S → P & ~U	~P/U → ~S
H → J & U	~J/~U → ~H

Combining conditional rules

Conditional rules chain together whenever a statement on the right of one conditional implies a statement on the left of another. For example, the conditional I → H & ~P chains together with H → J & U to yield I → H & J & U & ~P. This conditional, in turn, chains with S → P & ~U [more easily seen from the contrapositive: ~P/U → ~S] to yield I → H & J & U & ~P & ~S. In short, placing I in the C-group allows for the placement of every remaining element except for L. Some test takers prefer to explore these connections before turning to the items of a game; others rely on their previous experience with conditional rules to help them spot important consequences as they are needed when solving the items. Ultimately, one's approach to these rules will be a matter of personal preference, which will be informed and refined through practice with real logic games.

There is a subtle consequence of some of these rules that is worth mentioning, however. Although clever chaining of the rules would allow one to draw it, this consequence can be quickly identified by virtue of an easy-to-spot feature of the rules. Consider rules 2 and 3:

I → H & ~P

S → P & ~U

Notice that each of P and ~P is implied by the right of side of one of these rules. Obviously the element P can't be in both groups, so at most one of the elements I and S can be in the C-group. In other words, at least one of J and S must be in the not-C-group. A similar consequence involves rules 3 and 4:

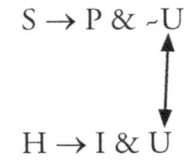

S → P & ~U

H → I & U

Key Strategies for Setting up Logic Games and Solving the Questions

At least one of S and H must be in the not-C group. These two consequences can be added directly to our diagram, using a slash for "or" as before. In general, the more information one can transfer from the rule into the diagram of the game, the better. The following, then, is the set-up for the present game, with original rules, their contrapositives, and the two additional consequences added to the diagram:

```
    S/H
    J/S
                L → I/S         ~I & ~S → ~L
 C  |  ~C
    |           I → H & ~P      ~H/P → ~I
    |
    |           S → P & ~U      ~P/U → ~S
    |
    |           H → J & U       ~J/~U → ~H
```

Elements of different types

- as with simple grouping, plus elements are sorted into types

A tour group will visit exactly five out of 10 sites. Three of the sites are <u>Anatolian</u>—B, C, and D—three of the sites are <u>Iranian</u>—F, G, and H—and four of the sites are <u>Macedonian</u>—P, Q, R, and S. The selection of visited sites must meet the following conditions:

The visited sites must include exactly one <u>Iranian</u> site.

B and D cannot both be visited.

H and S cannot both be visited.

P and Q cannot both be visited.

B cannot be visited unless S is also visited.

Q cannot be visited unless D is also visited.

31

This game is very similar to the previous game: two groups, V and not-V, with five elements in each. The most important difference is that the elements are of three different types – A, I, and M – and the rules refer to elements both by name and by type. A slight modification to the previous diagram, a row for each type of element, makes it easier to apply the rules, as well as to spot violations of them:

```
              (5)              (5)
               V                ~V
A
      BCD      _____|_____
I
      FGH      _____|_____
M
      PQRS               |
```

Rules 1 through 4 of this game can be represented naturally enough. We'll add a (1) to the I-V box to indicate that exactly one I-element is in V. Rules 2 through 4 are much like our derived consequences from the previous game: if B and D cannot both be in V, for instance, then at least one of B or D is in not-V. We'll use the slash for "or" as with the previous game, and add this to the top of the not-V column, and the same for the next two rules

The last two rules present a slight challenge – translating "unless" into conditional notation. The following rule is helpful:

"Not-A, unless B"   A → B

For example, "she doesn't go shopping unless there is a sale" becomes "if she goes shopping then there is a sale." In short, treat "unless" as an arrow, and add a negation to what is before the "unless."

On the LSAT, "unless" statements almost always have a negation in the first part already, so the net effect is to remove that negation. Thus our diagram, with all the rules and their contrapositives, looks like this:

```
                            P/Q
                            H/S
                            B/D

              (5)                    (5)
               V         |    ~V
    A    ─────────────────────────────        B → S      ~S → ~B
    BCD
    I                   (1)                   Q → D      ~D → ~Q
         ─────────────────────────────
    FGH
    M
    PQRS
```

There are a couple of small additional consequences that one might add to the diagram. Since there is only one I-element in V, four elements must come from A and M. But at most two can come from A (B or D must be in not-V), and at most three can come from M (P or Q must be in not-V). So one or two A-elements will be in V, and two or three M-elements will be in V.

33

Overlapping categories

- groups consist of two sets of overlapping categories

Exactly six aviators—Noonan, Quinn, Roberts, Sanchez, Torino, and Vega—are to constitute <u>three flight crews, A, B, and C</u>, each consisting of exactly <u>one pilot and one co-pilot</u>. Each aviator is on exactly one of the fight crews. The flight crews must be formed according to the following specifications:

Quinn is on the same flight crew as either Noonan or Torino.

Vega is a pilot, and Sanchez is on flight crew B.

Quinn is a pilot if and only if Roberts is not.

The important thing to notice about this stimulus is that it introduces two categories of groups: three flight crews, and two types of aviator, pilot and co-pilot. This key feature – two sets of overlapping categories – strongly suggests a grid diagram, with columns (for instance) corresponding to the three flight crews, and one row each for pilot and co-pilot:

```
         N Q R S T V
        ┌───┬───┬───┐
        │ A │ B │ C │
   P    │   │   │   │
        ├───┼───┼───┤
   C    │   │   │   │
        └───┴───┴───┘
```

The rules are easy enough to represent. Rule 1 places Q in a box with "N/T." We'll orient this box vertically to remind us that they share a column, rather than a row. Rule 2 places V in the P row, and S in the B column. Although rule 3 is written in bi-conditional form, in the two-group case such as this it has a clearer meaning: exactly one of Q and R is in each row. This allows us

Key Strategies for Setting up Logic Games and Solving the Questions

to represent rule 3 by placing Q/R in both the C row and the P row. Finally, we'll note one additional consequence: if either N or T is in Q's column, then they must be in different columns. We'll add this consequence to the rules.

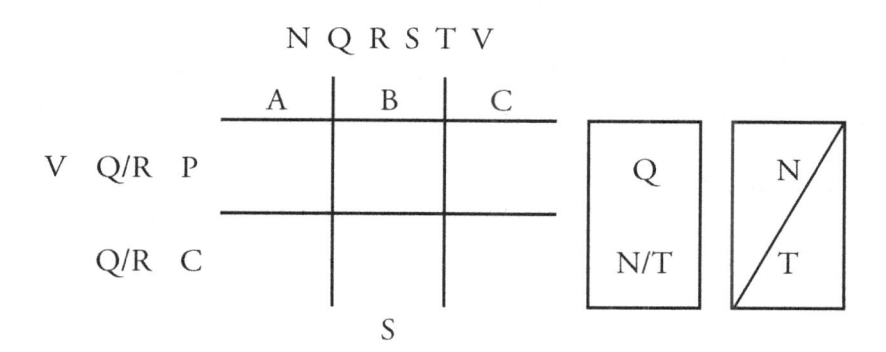

```
           N Q R S T V
         A   |  B  |  C
        ─────┼─────┼─────
V  Q/R  P    |     |          Q      N/
             |     |                 / 
        ─────┼─────┼─────   ─────   /───
Q/R  C       |     |          N/T   / T
             |     |
             S
```

Sequencing groups of elements

- elements are placed into groups, groups are sequenced

A four day music festival will feature six headlining bands—*Supa Menz, Tone Def, Vice Quad, Whine Iron, Youth Tunes,* and *Ziggurat*. Each band will play on exactly one day of the festival, and each day of the festival will feature at least one of the bands. The schedule of headlining bands must conform to the following conditions:

> No more than two of the bands will play on any day.
>
> *Vice Quad* will play on the day <u>immediately before</u> *Supa Menz*.
>
> Either *Supa Menz* or *Youth Sounds* will play on the <u>same day</u> as *Tone Def*.
>
> At most one of the bands will play on a day <u>after</u> *Whine Metal* plays.

35

Mastering LSAT Logic Games

The scenario of this stimulus is very similar to that of a simple grouping game – two categories of things, with the first serving as the names for collections of elements from the second. The rules, however, not only contain expressions that suggest grouping, such as "on the same day as," but ordering as well, as in "immediately before." So the days serve as groups, but these groups are themselves ordered sequentially. A quick check of the scenario reveals that each element occurs in exactly one group, and that each group contains at least one element. A simple grouping grid diagram with four columns will work here; the only difference is that elements are not only placed into groups, but ordered as well.

The rules of this game are all standard ordering and grouping rules; the only new wrinkle is that they occur together in the same game. Let's add to the diagram a few helpful consequences of the rules: since V is before S, S is not in group 1 and V is not in group 4. Since every group has at least one element, by rule 4 W is in group 3 or 4. And since T is in a group with another element, by rule 4 T is not in group 4. In spite of its apparent complexity, the items of this game should be easy to solve.

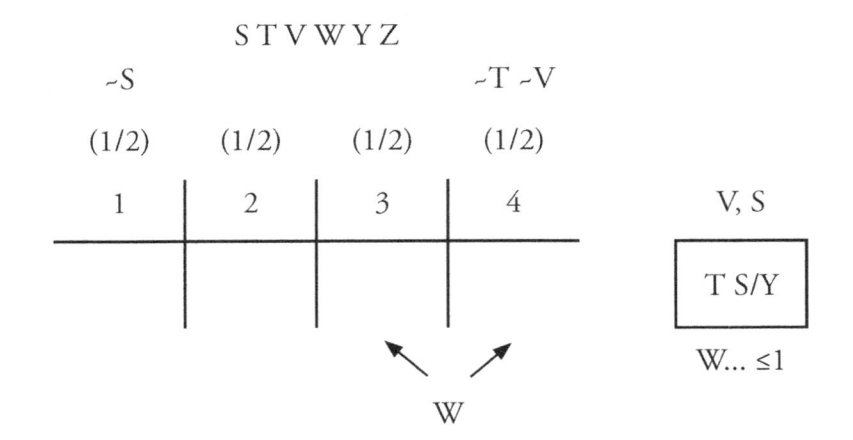

```
              S T V W Y Z
   ~S                        ~T ~V
  (1/2)    (1/2)    (1/2)    (1/2)
    1   |    2   |    3   |    4         V, S
        |        |        |
        |        |        |              ┌─────┐
        |        |        |              │ T S/Y │
                      ↖   ↗              └─────┘
                        W                W... ≤1
```

36

Key Strategies for Setting up Logic Games and Solving the Questions

Multiple groups, (some) elements sequenced

- elements are placed into groups, and ordered, individually

Six dishes—Filet, Gumbo, Halibut, Pesto, Quiche, Ravioli— are offered by a restaurant. Each dish is offered either at lunch or at dinner, but not both. The prices for the lunch dishes are 8, 9, and 10 dollars; while the prices for the dinner dishes are 9, 10, and 11 dollars. Each dish has exactly one price, and is offered by the restaurant consistent with the following conditions:

Pesto costs either 8 dollars or 9 dollars.

Gumbo costs less than Filet.

If Filet costs 10 dollars, then Ravioli does not.

Halibut is offered at dinner if, and only if, Ravioli is not.

Quiche costs one dollar more than Pesto, and the same as Gumbo.

This stimulus combines ordering and grouping in another natural way: six elements are placed individually into groups that are formed by the overlapping categories of meal (L or D) and price (8, 9, 10, or 11).

But elements are also ordered by price, as the expressions "costs less than" and "costs one dollar more than" in the rules indicate.

Let's use a variation on the "overlapping categories" diagram for this game, striking through the cells that contain no elements:

37

Mastering LSAT Logic Games

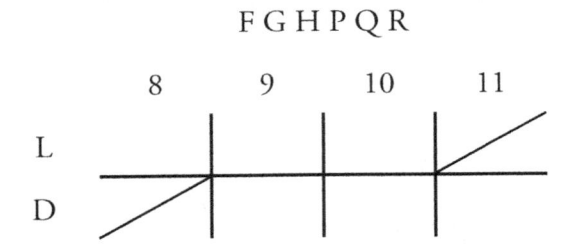

```
         F G H P Q R
        8   9   10   11
    L  ──┼───┼───┼──
    D  ──┼───┼───┼──
```

The rules again are all familiar from earlier games, even if their context is new.

One important change due to this new context is that "one position after" does not imply "in the same row as," as in standard sequencing games.

Rule 5, for example, simply requires Q to be in the column immediately to the right of P, not necessarily immediately after P in the same row.

Rules 1 and 5 combine in a nice way: since P is in column 8 or 9, Q and G are in 9 or 10. Here is the diagram with the rules and this additional consequence added:

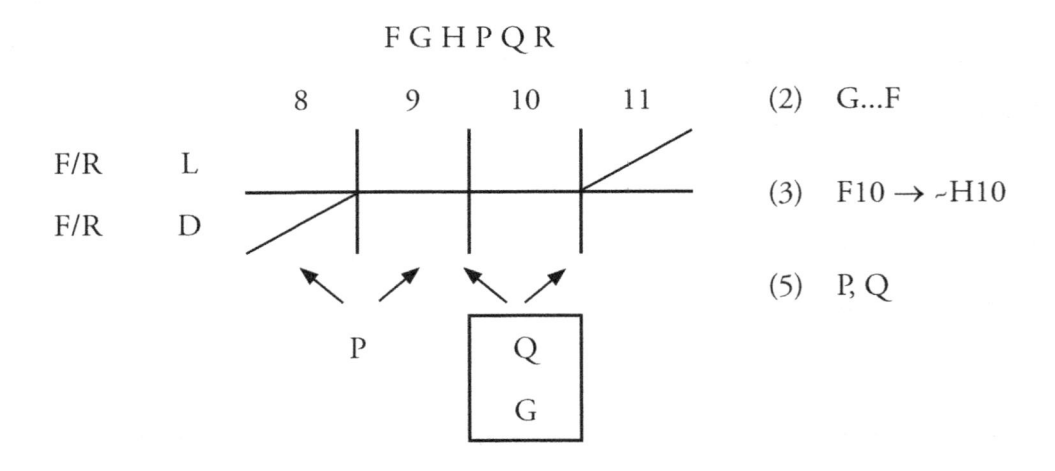

```
              F G H P Q R
             8   9   10   11           (2)  G...F
    F/R   L ──┼───┼───┼──
                                        (3)  F10 → ~H10
    F/R   D ──┼───┼───┼──
                ↖ ↗ ↖ ↗                 (5)  P, Q
                 P   ┌─────┐
                     │  Q  │
                     │  G  │
                     └─────┘
```

38

Sequencing categories/groups and elements

- as with sequencing groups, except both groups and group names sequenced

Five runners—Kennedy, Mottram, Rogers, Tergat, and Viren—will compete in three different heats of the same event at a track meet—<u>heats A, B, and C—but not necessarily in that order</u>. Each runner will compete in exactly one of the heats, and at least one of the runners will compete in each of the heats. The schedule of runners to heats must conform to the following requirements:

Heat A must take place <u>before</u> heat B.

Heat B includes Viren.

The heat that includes Komen must take place <u>before</u> any heat that includes either Mottram or Tergat.

The heat that includes Rogers cannot take place <u>after</u> any heat that includes Viren.

This stimulus is very similar to the sequencing groups game above, but with one addition: the group names must be sequenced as well, a fact reflected by rule 1. So the diagram for this game will resemble that of a simple grouping game or sequencing groups game, except that the group names are themselves treated as a separate category of elements to be sequenced:

```
A B C      __|__|__
K M R T V     |  |
```

The rules of this game combine grouping and sequencing in familiar ways. Rule 2, which places V in B, is easily represented by orienting a box containing them vertically. Rule 4, the last rule, is not equivalent to saying that R is before V, since it could be that R and V are in the same group.

The standard sequencing consequences apply: A cannot be in position 3 and B cannot be in position 1. In this case, with only three choices, it might be better to write this as "A/C" over position 1, and "B/C" over position 3. Similar facts apply to the bottom row: K cannot be in position 3 and M and T cannot be in position 1. Here's the diagram, with rules and these consequences added:

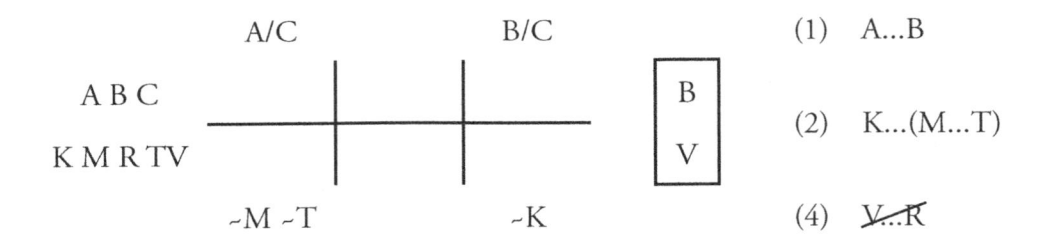

```
            A/C         B/C
  A B C      |           |           ┌───┐      (1)  A...B
            ─┼───────────┼─          │ B │
  K M R T V  |           |           │ V │      (2)  K...(M...T)
            -M -T        -K          └───┘
                                                (4)  ~~V...R~~
```

Setting up games, conclusion

These, then, are the most common game types found on the LSAT. Virtually all of the more than 200 released logic games are instances of one of the above nine game types, with minor variations.

The key to setting up games is *to get beneath the real-world veneer in the scenario that makes each game unique, and to focus on the roles played by the fundamental logical notions of ordering and grouping.* You'll be amazed at how familiar these games become with a little practice.

Of course, the best way to practice is with real AR stimuli from the LSAT PrepTest series from LSAC. Go to LSAC.org to find the complete PrepTest series.

Key Strategies for Setting up Logic Games and Solving the Questions

I wrote this book to be **timeless**, but I also want to make sure you get access to the **most effective** and **up-to-date tactics and strategies**.

I regularly update **LSATUnplugged.com** with new techniques as I develop and discover them.

"I fought my way to a 175 on the LSAT. Now, I want *you* to get a higher score!"

STEVE SCHWARTZ
Author

Solving Items

AR items come in sets of five to seven per stimulus. The majority of items come from one of two item families – the "could be true" family and the "must be true" family.

Could be true:

<u>If the minister from T rides in limousine 2, then</u> which one of the following <u>could ride in limousine 5?</u>

(A) The advisor from R
(B) The advisor from S
(C) The advisor from T
(D) The minister from R
(E) The minister from S

Conditional stem, focused stem

Must be true:

Which one of the following must be true?

(A) The advisor from R rides in limousine 2.
(B) The advisor from S rides in limousine 3.
(C) The advisor from S rides in limousine 4.
(D) The minister from R rides in limousine 4.
(E) The minister from S rides in limousine 5.

Categorical stem, unfocused stem

The item on the left asks about what could happen given the rules, and so is a "could be true" item. The item on the right, on the other hand, asks about what must happen given the rules, and so is a "must be true" item. These notions, while related, require that we approach these two types of items differently – what is a sound approach to one item type is not to the other. Nonetheless, the two families of strategies that we'll develop for these item types will involve similar steps: checking the rules, working through the answer choices, etc. The key is understanding how the different goals of each item type require a different implementation of each step.

Key Strategies for Setting up Logic Games and Solving the Questions

There are two other important differences between these two items, differences that are independent of the "could be true/must be true" distinction. Intuitively, the stem on the left is much more helpful than is the stem on the right. This is due to two features of the stem, one "on the way in," as it where, and the other "on the way out." Notice that the stem on the left is a conditional statement, and so we'll call it a *conditional stem*. This is obviously helpful, in that the item itself furnishes us with additional information that we can use to solve it, much like a mini-rule for use on this item only. Not so the stem on the right. This item must be solved on the basis of the rules alone, and so we'll call it a *categorical stem*.

The other difference is subtler. The stem on the left lets us know precisely what to look for, the occupant of limousine 5. This focus on a particular aspect of the game allows us to attend to specific features of the rules while solving it, making it more likely that we'll be able to determine a possible answer first, and check it against the answer choices second. We'll call a stem that contains this kind of information about the fact we're looking for a *focused stem*. The stem on the right, by contrast, simply states that we're looking for something that must be true, with no hint as to what other characteristics this fact might have. Here it is less likely that attending to the rules first will be helpful, since one has no idea which aspects of the rules one should attend to. Items such as this with an *unfocused stem* are often most efficiently solved by working through the answer choices. We'll show how to implement these suggestions once we outline our item-solving strategies and turn to some practice items.

The "could be true" family

The "could be true" item family consists of two types of items – "could be true" items and "must be false" items:

If the minister from T rides in limousine 2, then which one of the following could ride in limousine 5?

(A) The advisor from R   correct answer choice *could be true*
(B) The advisor from S
(C) The advisor from T   so incorrect answer choices *must be false*
(D) The minister from R
(E) The minister from S

Which one of the following statements must be false?

(A) The advisor from R rides in limousine 3.   correct answer choice *must be false*
(B) The minister from S rides in limousine 3.
(C) The advisor from T rides in limousine 1   so incorrect answer choices *could be true*
(D) The advisor from S rides in limousine 5
(E) The minister from T rides in limousine 6.

Notice that for both types of items, all of the answer choices fall into two categories: either they could be true, or else they must be false. The only difference between these two item types is how many answer choices fit into each category. For "could be true" items, one answer choice could be true while four must be false. For "must be false" items, it is exactly the other way around – one answer choice must be false, while four could be true.

It is the fact that every answer choice is of one or the other of these two types that makes "could be true" and "must be false" items so closely related: in either case we sort answer choices into the same two boxes; we just pick the contents of the different box for a "could be true" item than we do for a "must be false" item.

What do we mean by "could be true" **and "must be false?"** To say that an answer choice could be true is to say that there is an arrangement of elements that satisfies all of the rules, and which makes the answer choice true. Conversely, to say that an answer choice must be false is to say that any arrangement of elements that makes the answer choice true breaks at least one of the rules. Both of these facts are relevant. For both members of the "could be true" family both approaches will be helpful - recognizing when an answer choice is possible, as well as recognizing when an answer choice breaks the rules. In fact, each of these facts suggests its own strategy for members of the "could be true" family.

Item solving strategies for the "could be true" family:

CBT1: use the rules to recognize when answer choices break them.

CBT2: try to make answer choices true by constructing arrangements of elements that satisfy all of the rules.

Intuitively, CBT1 is a rule-focused strategy, while CBT2 is an answer-choice focused strategy. In practice any such division is slightly artificial, in that one will likely blend the two into an integrated approach when working on most items. But the theoretical distinction is essential to a clear understanding of precisely what one should do at each step of the item-solving process.

Notice, for instance, that for any given item, one of the strategies will be an indirect strategy employing the process of elimination, while the other will allow one to recognize the correct answer directly. But which strategy serves which purpose depends on which kind of item one is solving – with "could be true" items, for example, CBT1 is an elimination strategy while CBT2 is the direct strategy; but for "must be false" items CBT1 is the direct strategy and CBT2 is an elimination strategy.

More importantly, for items that have conditional stems, or stems that are focused, working with the rules sooner rather than later-CBT1-is often the most efficient approach; while with items that have categorical, unfocused stems, one often one finds that working through the answer choices-CBT2-is more efficient.

Let's illustrate these strategies with a game.

Item solving strategies for the "could be true" family: example

Six diplomats – a foreign minister and a senior advisor from each of three countries, R, S, and T – travel by limousine from their hotel to a meeting. Six limousines numbered 1 through 6 arrive at the hotel, and exactly one diplomat enters each limousine. The limousines then depart for the meeting one at a time, in numerical order. The assignment of diplomats to limousines is governed by the following conditions:

    The diplomats in the first two limousines to depart are from the same country.

    The diplomat in limousine 3 is from a different country
    than the diplomat in limousine 4.

    Limousines 1 and 4 each carry either the foreign minister
    from R or the senior advisor from T.

    The senior advisor from S is not in the last limousine to depart.

Key Strategies for Setting up Logic Games and Solving the Questions

A sequencing approach to this game seems natural enough. On this approach the elements correspond to the six diplomats, who we can refer to by means of a capital letter for the country and a lower case letter for the rank of each. Positions in the sequence then correspond to the number of the limousine each diplomat departs in.

A natural way to represent the rules is to label the diagram directly. We'll use "=" and "≠" between positions in the sequence to represent rules 1 and 2. For rules 3 and 4 we'll and use "/" for "or" and "~" for "not" and place the appropriate expressions beneath the indicated positions. This approach yields the following set-up:

```
____ = ____  ____ ≠ ____  ____  ____
Rm/Ta         Rm/Ta        ~Sa
```

Now, let's consider this first item, a "could be true" item.

1. Which one of the following could list the order in which the diplomats depart the hotel, from first to last?

   (A) minister from R, advisor from R, minister from T, minister from S, advisor from T, advisor from S

   (B) minister from T, advisor from S, minister from S, minister from R, advisor from T, advisor from R

   (C) advisor from R, minister from R, advisor from S, minister from T, advisor for T, minister for S

   (D) advisor from T, minister from T, minister from S, minister from R, advisor from S, advisor from R

   (E) advisor from T, minister from T, advisor from R, minister from R, advisor from S, minister from S

Mastering LSAT Logic Games

This item has a distinctive feature that provides a strong clue as to how to solve it: the answer choices each consist of complete assignments of elements to positions. With "could be true" items such as this, often the most efficient approach is to take the rules one at a time, and eliminate any answer choices that violate them - CBT1.

We can start in any order we like; let's start with Rm or Ta in position 1. Answer choice B places Tm in position 1, while C places Ra in position 1. (See item and diagram below.) These answer choices violate this rule, and can be eliminated; they must be false.

Rm or Ta in position 4 eliminates answer choice A. The rule "positions 1 and 2 from the same country" does not eliminate any remaining answer choices, so let's move to "positions 3 and 4 from different countries." Answer choice E places both R elements in positions 3 and 4, and so can be eliminated. All four of the "must be false" answer choices have been identified; only answer choice D remains, so it could be true. The correct answer is D.

1. Which one of the following could list the order in which the diplomats depart the hotel, from first to last?

    (A) minister from R, advisor from R, minister from T, minister from S, advisor from T, advisor from S

    (B) minister from T, advisor from S, minister from S, minister from R, advisor from T, advisor from R

    (C) advisor from R, minister from R, advisor from S, minister from T, advisor for T, minister for S

    (D) advisor from T, minister from T, minister from S, minister from R, advisor from S, advisor from R

    (E) advisor from T, minister from T, advisor from R, minister from R, advisor from S, minister from S

Key Strategies for Setting up Logic Games and Solving the Questions

___ = ___   ___ ≠ ___   ___   ___

[Rm/Ta]   [Rm/Ta]   ~Sa

Notice, we know that answer choice D could be true not because we understand how it could be true, but because we've identified four answer choices that must be false, so D must be the correct answer. Although it isn't necessary to verify that D could be true, it is easily done by plugging in the elements as assigned:

Ta = Tm   Sm ≠ Rm   Sa   Ra
___   ___   ___ ___
Rm/Ta   Rm/Ta   ~Sa

Since the above arrangement satisfies all of the rules and makes answer choice D true, D could be true, and so is the correct answer.

Now let's look at another item:

2. Which one of the following statements must be false?

(A) The advisor from R rides in limousine 3.
(B) The minister from S rides in limousine 3.
(C) The advisor from T rides in limousine 1.
(D) The advisor from S rides in limousine 5.
(E) The minister from T rides in limousine 6.

Item 2 is a categorical "must be false" item with an unfocused stem. A quick scan of the answer choices shows that they are all statements to the effect that a particular element is in a particular position. It is possible that, having drawn consequences from the rules that required certain elements to be in certain positions, we could solve this item by attending to these consequences, and then checking for an answer choice that contradicted one of them (CBT1). But in the present case, with no such consequences drawn, focusing on the rules first seems inefficient. We're probably better off working through the answer choices by plugging them in to see if they describe possible arrangements (CBT2).

Consider answer choice A. Place Ra in position 3:

___ = ___   Ra ≠ ___   ___   ___

Rm/Ta   Rm/Ta   ~Sa

By the facts indicated by the boxes, Ta must be in position 4:

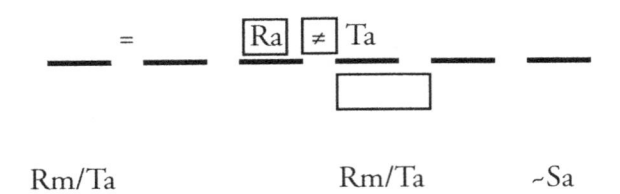

___ = ___   [Ra] ≠ Ta ___   ___
              [   ]

Rm/Ta   Rm/Ta   ~Sa

But then, Rm must be in position 1, as shown in red. This in turn requires another R-element for position 2, as shown in blue:

[Rm] = ?   Ra ≠ [Ta] ___   ___

[Rm/Ta]   Rm/Ta   ~Sa

Key Strategies for Setting up Logic Games and Solving the Questions

But there are no R-elements remaining – they already occupy positions 1 and 3. Thus, placing Ra in position 3 breaks the rules, and so answer choice A must be false. The correct answer is A.

But then, answer choices B – E could be true, as is easily verified by plugging them in. Let's try answer choice B:

Rm = Ra	Sm ≠ Ta	Sa	Tm
Rm/Ta	Rm/Ta	~Sa	

This arrangement of elements makes answer choice B true while satisfying all of the rules. Thus answer choice B could be true, and can be eliminated. The same can be done for C-E. Of course, as soon as we find one answer choice that breaks the rules, we have solved this item; there is no need to show that the remaining answer choices could be true. Still, sometimes one will try out another answer choice or two before moving on to the next item just to make sure than one hasn't made a mistake.

Let's try another item:

3. If the minister from T rides in limousine 2, then which one of the following statements could be true?

   (A) The advisor from R rides in limousine 4.

   (B) The advisor from R rides in limousine 5.

   (C) The minister from S rides in limousine 1.

   (D) The advisor from S rides in neither limousine 3 nor limousine 5.

   (E) Neither diplomat from S rides in limousine 3.

Item 3 is a conditional "could be true" item with an unfocused stem. The first step is to add the condition from the stem to the diagram, and see what consequences can be drawn (CBT1). This should be familiar from the previous item:

$$\underline{\quad\quad} = \text{Tm} \quad \underline{\quad\quad} \neq \underline{\quad\quad} \quad \underline{\quad\quad} \quad \underline{\quad\quad}$$
Rm/Ta · · · · · · · · · · · · · · Rm/Ta · · · · ~Sa

By the facts indicated, Ta is in position 1:

$$\underline{\text{Ta}} \;\boxed{=\;\text{Tm}}\; \underline{\quad\quad} \neq \underline{\quad\quad} \quad \underline{\quad\quad} \quad \underline{\quad\quad}$$
$\boxed{\text{Rm/Ta}}$ · · · · · · · · · · · Rm/Ta · · · · ~Sa

But then Rm is in position 4:

$$\boxed{\text{Ta}} = \text{Tm} \quad \underline{\quad\quad} \neq \text{Rm} \quad \underline{\quad\quad}$$
Rm/Ta · · · · · · · · · · · $\boxed{\text{Rm/Ta}}$ · · · · ~Sa

At this stage additional consequences are hard to draw, and so the next step is to check the diagram against the answer choices, seeing which of them are made false by the stem condition and the resulting consequences:

3. If the minister from T rides in limousine 2, then which one of the following statements could be true?

   (A) The advisor from R rides in limousine 4.
   (B) The advisor from R rides in limousine 5.
   (C) The minister from S rides in limousine 1.

(D) The advisor from S rides in neither limousine 3 nor limousine 5.

(E) Neither diplomat from S rides in limousine 3.

In fact, the partial arrangement above makes answer choices A and C, false, and so they can be eliminated; no matter how we complete the assignment of elements to positions these answer choices will remain false.

CBT1 has allowed us to identify and eliminate two of the four incorrect answer choices; now it's time to switch strategies and work through the remaining answer choices - CBT2. Let's try answer choice B, and place Ra in position 5:

$$\underline{\quad\quad} = \underline{\quad\quad} \quad \underline{\quad\quad} \neq \underline{\quad\quad} \quad \underline{\text{Ra}} \quad \underline{\quad\quad}$$

Rm/Ta Rm/Ta ~Sa

This, then, requires Ta and Tm to occupy positions 1 and 2…

$$\underline{\text{Ta}} \boxed{=} \underline{\text{Tm}} \quad \underline{\quad\quad} \neq \underline{\quad\quad} \quad \underline{\text{Ra}} \quad \underline{\quad\quad}$$

$\boxed{\text{Rm/Ta}}$ Rm/Ta ~Sa

…which then requires Rm to go in position 4:

$$\boxed{\text{Ta}} = \underline{\text{Tm}} \quad \underline{\quad\quad} \neq \underline{\text{Rm}} \quad \underline{\text{Ra}} \quad \underline{\quad\quad}$$

Rm/Ta $\boxed{\text{Rm/Ta}}$ ~Sa

Complete the assignment by placing the S-elements, being sure not to place Sa in position 6:

Ta = Tm	Sa ≠ Rm	Ra	Sm
Rm/Ta		Rm/Ta		|-Sa|

This arrangement of elements satisfies all of the rules and makes answer choice B true. So the correct answer is B. This solution illustrates how often one will combine strategies when solving items, which is the key to efficient use of time.

4. Which one of the following statements could be true?

(A) The advisor from R rides in limousine 1.

(B) The minister from T rides in limousine 1.

(C) The minister from S rides in limousine 1, and the secretary from T rides in limousine 5.

(D) The advisor from T rides in limousine 1, and the minister from T rides in limousine 2.

(E) The advisor from T rides in limousine 1, and neither diplomat from S rides in limousine 3.

This is a categorical "could be true" item with an unfocused stem, and so attending to the answer choices first is probably the best approach. But this item illustrates a common situation – when we look at the answer choices with one eye on the rules, we can quickly identify several that break them without having to go to the trouble of actually plugging them in.

Key Strategies for Setting up Logic Games and Solving the Questions

Notice, for instance, that answer choices A, B, and C all place an element in position 1. Our diagram tells us a lot about this position - by the "Rm/Ta" rule, only one of these two elements can occupy it. But in fact none of these answer choices involves either of them!

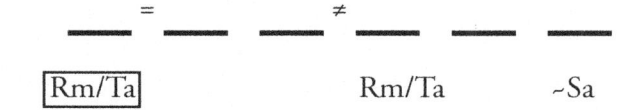

$$\underline{} \stackrel{=}{} \underline{} \stackrel{\neq}{} \underline{} \underline{} \underline{}$$

$\boxed{\text{Rm/Ta}}$ Rm/Ta   ~Sa

4. Which one of the following statements could be true?

(A̶) The advisor from R rides in limousine 1.

(B̶) The minister from T rides in limousine 1.

(C̶) The minister from S rides in limousine 1, and the secretary from T rides in limousine 5.

(D) The advisor from T rides in limousine 1, and the minister from T rides in limousine 2.

(E) The advisor from T rides in limousine 1, and neither diplomat from S

While D and E also involve position 1, they each place an acceptable element there. Thus evaluating these answer choices will be more involved than simply spotting an immediate violation of the rules, and so CBT2 in it's more robust sense will probably have to be employed here. Let's try Answer choice D, and place Ta in position 1 and Tm in position 2:

$$\underset{\text{Rm/Ta}}{\underline{\text{Ta}}} \stackrel{=}{} \underset{}{\underline{\text{Tm}}} \stackrel{\neq}{} \underline{} \underset{\text{Rm/Ta}}{\underline{}} \underset{\text{~Sa}}{\underline{}}$$

55

Now, any way of completing the sequence that satisfies the rules will be enough to make answer choice D true. There are several ways to finish; here's one way:

Ta = Tm   Sa ≠ Rm   Ra   Sm
‾‾‾‾‾‾‾‾   ‾‾‾‾‾‾‾‾   ‾‾   ‾‾
Rm/Ta   Rm/Ta   ~Sa

Thus answer choice D could be true, and so the correct answer is D.

These two strategies, CBT1 and CBT2, can be used either alone or in combination to solve roughly half of the items on the test. CBT1, focusing on the rules, is often the fastest approach when one sees how they apply to a given item, as when the stem is focused. But when all else fails, it will always be possible to solve an item from the "could be true" family by plugging in answer choices, or CBT2. While perhaps less elegant and more time-consuming than focusing on the rules, CBT2 is an all-purpose strategy that will never let you down.

The "must be true" family

The "must be true" item family consists of two types of items – "must be true" items and "could be false" items:

If the minister from T rides in limousine 6, then which one of the following statements must be true?

(A) The advisor from S rides in limousine 3.   correct answer choice *must be true*
(B) The advisor from S rides in limousine 5.
(C) The minister from S rides in limousine 5.   so incorrect answer choices *could be false*
(D) The advisor from R rides in limousine 2.
(E) The minister from R rides in limousine 2

Key Strategies for Setting up Logic Games and Solving the Questions

If the advisor from T rides in limousine 1, Then which one of the following statements could be false?

(A) The advisor from R rides in limousine 3.   correct answer choice *could be false*
(B) The minister from S rides in limousine 3.
(C) The advisor from T rides in limousine 1   so incorrect answer choices *must be true*
(D) The advisor from S rides in limousine 5
(E) The minister from T rides in limousine 6.

Again, for both types of items, all of the answer choices fall into two categories: either they must be true, or else they could be false. The only difference between these two item types is how many answer choices fit into each category. For "must be true" items, one answer choice must be true while four could be false; for "could be false" items, one answer choice could be false while four must be true.

Once more, it is the fact that every answer choice is of one or the other of these two types that makes "must be true" and "could be false" items closely related: in either case we sort answer choices into the same two boxes; we just pick the contents of the different box for a "must be true" item than we do for a "could be false" item.

What do we mean by "must be true" and "could be false?" To say that an answer choice must be true is to say that it follows as a consequence of the rules. Conversely, to say that an answer choice could be false is to say that it is possible to *make the answer choice false without violating the rules*.

This last point is crucial, and will have a direct bearing on our item-solving strategies: in order to evaluate an answer choice from a member of the "must be true" family one must try to *make it false*!

Mastering LSAT Logic Games

Again, corresponding to each of these notions, we have an item-solving strategy.

Item solving strategies for the "must be true" family:

MBT1: use the rules to recognize when answer choices follow from them.

MBT2: try to make answer choices *false* by constructing arrangements of elements that satisfy all of the rules.

As with CBT1 and CBT2, the first strategy is rule-focused, while the second is answer-choice focused. And as with the previous two strategies, in practice one will blend the two into an integrated approach to solving items.

The biggest difference between the two sets of strategies concerns the efficiency of MBT2: while evaluating answer choices by "plugging them in" (CBT2) is reasonably quick, evaluating them by trying to make them false can be a very time-consuming process. This is because often there will be several different ways to make an answer choice false, and all of them may have to be checked before we can reach an evaluative conclusion. We'll illustrate this point shortly. Let's turn to some items:

5. If the minister from T rides in limousine 6, then which one of the following statements must be true?

 (A) The advisor from S rides in limousine 3.
 (B) The advisor from S rides in limousine 5.
 (C) The minister from S rides in limousine 5.
 (D) The advisor from R rides in limousine 2.
 (E) The minister from S rides in limousine 3.

Key Strategies for Setting up Logic Games and Solving the Questions

This is a conditional "must be true" item. As with "could be true" items, a conditional stem usually allows one to draw additional consequences. Let's place Tm in position 6:

```
 ___  =  ___    ≠  ___   ___   ___   Tm
Rm/Ta         Rm/Ta          ~Sa
```

The next consequence is subtle, and some test takers may miss it. If you spot it, then working with the rules, MBT1, will lead you straight to the correct answer. Notice that positions 1 and 2 must be occupied by elements with the same first letter, and that position 1 must be occupied by either an R-element or a T-element. But there are no longer two T-elements available for positions 1 and 2, since one of these – Tm - occupies position 6. Thus Rm and Ra occupy positions 1 and 2, respectively:

```
 Rm | = | Ra    ≠  ___   ___   ___   [Tm]
[Rm/Ta]        Rm/Ta          ~Sa
```

Having drawn this consequence, a check of the answer choices reveals that answer choice D – the advisor from R rides in limousine 2 - is made true by it, and so it follows from the rules. Thus the correct answer is D.

On the other hand, suppose that this tricky consequence escaped us. Then we would have tried working through the answer choices, MBT2, instead. Let's start with answer choice A. This answer choice places Sa in position 3. Our goal is to try to make this false, let's place Sa in, say, position 5:

```
 ___  =  ___    ≠  ___   ___   Sa   Tm
Rm/Ta         Rm/Ta          ~Sa
```

59

Mastering LSAT Logic Games

Now let's fill in the rest of the elements around these, attending to the rules as we do, so as to make sure that we don't violate them:

$$\underline{Rm = Ra} \quad \underline{Sm \neq Ta} \quad \underline{Sa} \quad \underline{Tm}$$
$$Rm/Ta \qquad\qquad Rm/Ta \quad \sim Sa$$

Since this assignment of elements to positions satisfies all of the rules and makes answer choice A false, we can eliminate A. But before moving on to answer choice B, check to see if this arrangement makes any of the other answer choices false. In fact, answer choice C is made false by this arrangement as well, so we can also eliminate C:

5. If the minister from T rides in limousine 6, then which one of the following statements must be true?

   (A) The advisor from S rides in limousine 3.
   (B) The advisor from S rides in limousine 5.
   (C) The minister from S rides in limousine 5.
   (D) The advisor from R rides in limousine 2.
   (E) The minister from S rides in limousine 3.

Now let's try answer choice B. One way to make B false is simply to have Sa and Sm switch positions in the arrangement above:

$$\underline{Rm = Ra} \quad \underline{Sa \neq Ta} \quad \underline{Sm} \quad \underline{Tm}$$
$$Rm/Ta \qquad\qquad Rm/Ta \quad \sim Sa$$

60

This arrangement not only makes answer choice B false; it makes E false as well! Just like that, we have eliminated all four incorrect answer choices, and so the correct answer must be D.

5. If the minister from T rides in limousine 6, then which one of the following statements must be true?

(A) The advisor from S rides in limousine 3.

(B) The advisor from S rides in limousine 5.

(C) The minister from S rides in limousine 5.

(D) The advisor from R rides in limousine 2.

(E) The minister from S rides in limousine 3.

This item illustrates a couple of very important points: first, there is no "right way" to solve an item – how you will go about solving a particular item depends to a large degree on how much insight into the item you have. If an item has a focused stem, or if you have noticed several interesting consequences of the rules, then a rule-based approach such as MBT1 may be most efficient. But even if insight is utterly lacking, methodically working through the answer choices – MBT2 – will get you to the solution sooner or later.

The second point is that a big part of finding the solution sooner rather than later is making clever use of arrangements of elements used to evaluate answer choices. There is no need to reinvent the wheel – often one arrangement will be helpful on more than one answer choice. In fact, this observation is so important that we will soon develop it into a new item-solving strategy for each of our two item families.

6. If the advisor from T rides in limousine 1, Then which one of the following statements could be false?

    (A) The minister from R rides in limousine 4.

    (B) The minister from S rides in limousine 3.

    (C) The minister from T rides in limousine 2.

    (D) A diplomat from S rides in limousine 5 or 6.

    (E) A diplomat from R rides in limousine 5 or 6.

This is a "could be false" item; the correct answer can be made false without violating the rules, while the four incorrect answer choices will follow from the rules. Notice that, in this context, MBT1 is the indirect elimination strategy, while MBT2 is the direct solution strategy. Place Ta in position 1:

```
Ta    =          ≠
___   ___   ___   ___   ___   ___
Rm/Ta       Rm/Ta       ~Sa
```

With any luck we'll be able to draw enough consequences from the stem condition to eliminate some, if not all, of the incorrect answer choices. To begin with, Tm must occupy position 2:

```
[Ta] = [Tm]       ≠
___   ___   ___   ___   ___   ___
Rm/Ta       Rm/Ta       ~Sa
```

So then Rm must be in position 4:

```
[Ta] =  Tm        ≠  Rm
___   ___   ___   ___   ___   ___
Rm/Ta       [Rm/Ta]     ~Sa
```

Key Strategies for Setting up Logic Games and Solving the Questions

These are the obvious consequences that involve placing particular elements into positions, so let's check the answer choices:

6. If the advisor from T rides in limousine 1, Then which one of the following statements could be false?

   (A) The minister from R rides in limousine 4.
   (B) The minister from S rides in limousine 3.
   (C) The minister from T rides in limousine 2.
   (D) A diplomat from S rides in limousine 5 or 6.
   (E) A diplomat from R rides in limousine 5 or 6.

Answer choices A and C are made true by the consequences we've drawn, and so they must be true. We can eliminate A and C.

At this point a clever test taker might make the following observations: with only three spaces left and two S-elements, there aren't enough places to put them both if you can't use positions 5 and 6, so D must be true. And positions 5 and 6 are the only remaining allowable positions for Ra, so E must be true as well. Thus answer choice B is correct.

More likely, one would have missed these subtle consequences, or spent too much time drawing them, and would have been better served by switching to MBT2, working through the answer choices. Consider answer choice B. Let's try to make B false by placing Sm in position 5:

$$\underline{Ta} \quad = \quad \underline{Tm} \quad \quad \underline{} \quad \neq \quad \underline{Rm} \quad \underline{Sm} \quad \underline{}$$

$$Rm/Ta Rm/Ta \sim Sa$$

63

We have two elements to place and only one way to place them:

```
Ta  =  Tm     Sa [≠] Rm    Sm      Ra
___    ___    ___    ___   ___    ___
Rm/Ta         Rm/Ta                [~Sa]
```

This arrangement satisfies all of the rules and makes answer choice B false. So the correct answer is B, after all! This item shows how sometimes using the two strategies in concert will be more efficient than relying solely on one or the other: follow the consequences as far as you can, eliminate, and then switch to working through any remaining answer choices if you must.

Using possible arrangements of elements

Our second solution to item 5 above, the one employing MBT2, was made more efficient by using a single arrangement of elements to eliminate more than one answer choice.

This technique of using possible arrangements of elements can be greatly expanded, to the point that an arrangement from one item may help one solve other items from the same game. We'll illustrate this technique with one of the sequencing games from above:

> Seven job applicants—B, C, D, F, G, H, and J—are each scheduled
> For exactly one interview on the same day. The interviews are
> scheduled sequentially, one at a time. The order in which the
> interviews are scheduled is governed by the following conditions:
>
> > C must be scheduled before H.
> >
> > J must be scheduled immediately after D.
> >
> > B cannot be scheduled immediately before or immediately after D.

Key Strategies for Setting up Logic Games and Solving the Questions

F must be scheduled after D and before C.

G must be scheduled immediately before B.

Recall the set-up of this game, with the rules combined into a super-rule, and the diagram labeled with additional consequences:

B C D F G H J

...G, B

D, J...F...C...H

D   J

___ ___ ___ ___ ___ ___

                                      B/H

Next, consider this item:

1. If F is scheduled third, then which one of the following could be true?

    (A) B is scheduled fourth.

    (B) C is scheduled fifth.

    (C) C is scheduled sixth.

    (D) H is scheduled fourth.

    (E) H is scheduled sixth.

Let's place F in position 3:

B C D F G H J

...G, B

D, J...F...C...H

```
D    J    F    ___  ___  ___  ___
                              B/H
```

Notice that this requires that the G-B pair follow F, with C and H, in that order, mixed in. There are so few ways to arrange the remaining elements that we might as well list them all:

        C   H   G   B   ...G, B

        C   G   B   H   D, J...F...C...H

```
D    J    F    G    B    C    H
                              B/H
```

It is now easy to identify the correct answer from our diagram; the correct answer is C, as the bottom arrangement makes clear.

Now let's look at another item from the same game:

2. Which one of the following must be false?

    (A) B is scheduled fifth.

    (B) B is scheduled sixth.

    (C) C is scheduled fourth.

    (D) F is scheduled fourth.

    (E) H is scheduled fifth.

Key Strategies for Setting up Logic Games and Solving the Questions

This is a categorical "must be false" item with an unfocused stem. One's default approach to this item is probably to work through the answer choices, CBT2, and to eliminate those that are made true by one arrangement or another. But rather than trying to construct possible arrangements based on the answer choices, let's just use the three we already have, and see if they make any of the answer choices of this item true:

              C   H   G   B   …G, B

              C   G   B   H   D, J…F…C…H

D   J   F   G   B   C   H
‾   ‾   ‾   ‾   ‾   ‾   ‾
                                         B/H

In fact, answer choices A, B, C, and E are all made true by at least one of these arrangements, and so they can be eliminated:

2. Which one of the following must be false?

   (~~A~~) B is scheduled fifth.
   (~~B~~) B is scheduled sixth.
   (~~C~~) C is scheduled fourth.
   (D) F is scheduled fourth.
   (~~E~~) H is scheduled fifth.

D is the only remaining answer choice, so the correct answer is D! With practice, using possible arrangements can become the most efficient approach to many items.

Mastering LSAT Logic Games

Here's another item:

3. Which one of the following must be true?

    (A) At most one interview is between C's and H's.

    (B) At most two interviews are between G's and H's.

    (C) At most three interviews are between F's and H's.

    (D) At least one interview is between F's and G's.

    (E) At least three interviews are between J's and B's.

This is a categorical "must be true" item with an unfocused stem, another item type whose solution frequently requires working through the answer choices. As with the item above, possible arrangements serve to eliminate answer choices; but unlike the item above, answer choices to this "must be true" item can be eliminated when arrangements make them *false*, rather than true.

At first, the answer choices to this item appear daunting; not only do we have to contend with the meaning of, for instance, "at most one…," we also have to negate it. But the answer choices of this "must be true" item illustrate a common property of such answer choices generally: although the answer choice itself is complicated, its negation is not.

Consider answer choice A: at most one interview is between C's and H's. The way to make this false is to place two or more positions between C and H. Notice that this is exactly what the second, blue arrangement does, and so answer choice A can be eliminated:

    C   H   G   B   …G, B

    C   G   B   H   D, J…F…C…H

Key Strategies for Setting up Logic Games and Solving the Questions

D	J	F	G	B	C	H
_	_	_	_	_	_	_
						B/H

Continuing through the answer choices, we see that answer choice D is made false by the red arrangement, while answer choice E is made false by this arrangement as well:

3. Which one of the following must be true?

   (~~A~~) At most one interview is between C's and H's.

   (B) At most two interviews are between G's and H's.

   (C) At most three interviews are between F's and H's.

   (~~D~~) At least one interview is between F's and G's.

   (~~E~~) At least three interviews are between J's and B's.

So, we have eliminated three of the four incorrect answer choices, just by checking arrangements of elements from an earlier item! With only two answer choices remaining, it should be easy to finish using MBT2. Consider answer choice B. In order for this to be false, three or more positions must separate G and H. Let's place G as far forward, and H as far backward, as we can:

...G, B

D, J...F...C...H

D	J	G	B	F	C	H
_	_	_	_	_	_	_
						B/H

This assignment of elements to positions satisfies all of the rules and makes answer choice B false, so B can be eliminated. The correct answer is C.

Let's summarize this new strategy: possible arrangements of elements show what can happen, so we can use them to show that answer choices either could be true (for members of the "could be true" family) or else could be false (for members of the "must be true" family). This will be most useful as an elimination strategy; that is, appealing to possible arrangements will tend to be most helpful in eliminating incorrect answer choices for "must be false" and "must be true" items.

A quick recap of our three strategies for each of the two main item families:

Item-solving strategies for the "could be true" family

CBT1: use the rules to recognize when answer choices break them.

CBT2: try to make answer choices true by constructing arrangements of elements that satisfy all of the rules.

CBT3: use possible arrangements of elements to identify answer choices that could be true.

Item-solving strategies for the "must be true" family

MBT1: use the rules to recognize when answer choices follow from them.

MBT2: try to make answer choices *false* by constructing arrangements of elements that satisfy all of the rules.

MBT3: use possible arrangements of elements to identify answer choices that could be false.

Key Strategies for Setting up Logic Games and Solving the Questions

It helps to keep in mind the structure of this scheme: the first two strategies,, CBT1 and MBT1, are rule-focused strategies; the second two, CBT2 and MBT2, are answer-choice focused; while the third two, CBT3 and MBT3, are possible-arrangement focused.

In practice, of course, items will often be solved most efficiently by blending these strategies into an integrated approach, as illustrated above.

You now have all the tools you need to solve about 90% of AR items, those of the "could be true" and "must be true" item families.

Rarer item types

A few AR items (usually about two per test) do not concern merely what could be true or must be true, but instead involve one or another of several variations on these themes. Let's quickly survey these additional item types.

Fixed elements/possible arrangements

Consider this next item, from the same sequencing game:

4. If F is scheduled third, then how many different schedules of interviews are possible?

    (A) two

    (B) three

    (C) four

(D) five

(E) six

Item 4 asks not about what can happen in some arrangement or other, but instead asks how many different arrangements of a particular kind there are; namely, those in which F is in position 3. The reasoning behind the solutions to these items was foreshadowed during our discussion of item 1 above, the conditional "could be true" item that placed F in position 3. Recall that we simply listed all of the remaining arrangements of elements consistent with the rules by moving the G-B pair systematically along the line:

			C	H	G	B		...G, B
			C	G	B	H		D, J...F...C...H
D	J	F	G	B	C	H		

___ ___ ___ ___ ___ ___ ___

                                                                              B/H

So there are three possible arrangements of elements with F in position 3. The correct answer is B. We'll look at some other examples of this item type later.

A closely related item is the "fixed elements" item. These items ask how many elements' positions are completely determined by the rules, and any additional stem conditions. In the present case, elements D and J are determined to be in positions 1 and 2, respectively, by the rules; while the stem places F in position 3. The positions of all of the remaining elements can change from one arrangement to the next, and so only these three elements are fixed.

Of course, these items can occur either in the context of an ordering game, as here, or in a grouping context, In either case the basic principles are the same: identify elements that are fixed, and systematically work through the remaining placement options.

Earliest/latest

Here's an item type that is a hybrid involving both notions from the "could be true" family:

5. The earliest that H's interview could be scheduled is

    (A) third
    (B) fourth
    (C) fifth
    (D) sixth
    (E) seventh

This item asks how early in the sequence an element can occur. This "earliest" item is a combination "could be true" and "must be false" item: to identify a position as earliest is to claim both that (i) the element could occur in that position, and that (ii) the element cannot occur in any earlier position. Considering answer choices involving earlier options first, and working towards later options, takes care of (ii) automatically.

Mastering LSAT Logic Games

The stem is focused - we only care about possible positions of H - so a check of the rules is in order. Our super-rule places four elements in front of H, making H no earlier than position 5:

...G, B

| D, J...F...C...H |

```
  D    J                              B/H
 ___  ___  ___  ___  ___  ___  ___
```

Eliminate answer choices A and B.

5. The earliest that H's interview could be scheduled is

    (A) third
    (B) fourth
    (C) fifth
    (D) sixth
    (E) seventh

Let's try C. The following assignment of elements to positions places H in position 5 while satisfying all of the rules:

```
  D    J    F    C    H    G    B
 ___  ___  ___  ___  ___  ___  ___
```

Thus the correct answer is C:

Key Strategies for Setting up Logic Games and Solving the Questions

5. The earliest that H's interview could be scheduled is

    (A) third
    (B) fourth
    (C) fifth
    (D) sixth
    (E) seventh

The grouping game versions of earliest/latest items are greatest/least items. These items ask about the greatest possible number of elements in a group, or the least possible number of elements in a group. The same basic principles apply: with "earliest" and "fewest" items, try small answer choices first; while with "latest" and" greatest number" items, try large numbers first.

Complete and accurate list

6. Which one of the following is a complete and accurate list of applicants any one of whom could be interviewed fifth?

    (A) B, F
    (B) F, G
    (C) B, F, G
    (D) B, G, H
    (E) B, F, G, H

Mastering LSAT Logic Games

"Complete and accurate list" items are among the easiest to solve; just be sure that the item is in fact of the "complete and accurate list" kind, and not a variation on the familiar "could be true" item type. Consider the following two item stems:

Which one of the following could be a complete and accurate list of the elements occupying group A?

Which one of the following is a complete and accurate list of the elements that could occupy group A?

The first stem is a common grouping "could be true" stem. Here the presence of the expression "complete and accurate list" serves to indicate that the correct answer will include *all and only* elements in the group, as opposed to a subset of these elements, for instance. Notice that "could" comes before "complete and accurate" in this stem.

The second stem, like the stem of item 6 above it, is not a "could be true" stem. (This point should be clear from the answer choices of the item - each of them contains multiple elements, but in any particular arrangement only one element can occupy position 5!) This stem instead asks for the set of elements that occupy group A (or position 5) *in some arrangement or other*, not any particular arrangement. Notice that "complete and accurate" comes before "could" in this stem.

Complete and accurate list items are easily solved by appealing to previous arrangements of elements, and then plugging in as necessary. Let's revisit the arrangements from above:

        C |H| G   B   …G, B

        C |G| B   H   D, J…F…C…H

Key Strategies for Setting up Logic Games and Solving the Questions

```
D    J    F    G    B    C    H
___  ___  ___  ___  ___  ___  ___
                         B/H
```

In these three arrangements the elements B, G, and H are in position 5, so we can eliminate any answer choice that lacks one or more of these:

6. Which one of the following is a complete and accurate list of applicants any one of whom could be interviewed fifth?

   (A̶) B, F
   (B̶) F, G
   (C̶) B, F, G
   (D) B, G, H
   (E) B, F, G, H

So it comes down to answer choice D or E. Notice that the only difference between them is the presence of F in answer choice E. At this stage the best approach is to see if we can place F in position 5:

```
D    J    G    B    F    C    H
___  ___  ___  ___  ___  ___  ___
```

Since this arrangement satisfies all of the rules, we can eliminate answer choice D, and the correct answer is E.

77

This completes our survey of AR item types. Familiarity with the strategies presented above, and a clear understanding of how to use them in concert to create an integrated approach to solving items, is the first step. Next comes practice!

Sample Games

Let's look at some items for a sequencing game we introduced above:

> A recent study rated six new car models-L, M, N, P, Q, and R-with respect to overall passenger safety. No two models received the same rating, and each of the six models received exactly one rating. The safety ratings assigned to the models by the study are consistent with the following conditions:
>
> Q received a higher safety rating than M.
> R received a safety rating one higher that P's safety rating.
> N received the fourth-highest safety rating.
> P received a higher safety rating than M.

Recall this game's set-up, with the rules combined and the diagram labeled:

L M N P Q R

R, P...N...M

Q...

N

___ ___ ___ ___ ___ ___

P/R   L/M

Key Strategies for Setting up Logic Games and Solving the Questions

Let's try this item:

1. Which one of the following could be an accurate list of the safety ratings assigned to the models, from the highest safety rating to the lowest?

   (A) Q, M, R, P, N, L
   (B) Q, R, P, L, N, M
   (C) R, P, L, N, Q, M
   (D) Q, P, R, N, M, L
   (E) L, Q, R, N, P, M

This is a categorical "could be true" item, with answer choices that consist of complete assignments of elements to positions. This kind of item can be solved efficiently by taking the rules one at a time and eliminating answer choices that violate them – CBT1.

The P/R-rule eliminates answer choices A and E, the N-rule eliminates answer choice B, and the sequencing rule eliminates answer choice D:

L M N P Q R

$\boxed{\text{R, P...N...M}}$

$\boxed{\text{N}}$ Q...

___ ___ ___ ___ ___ ___

$\boxed{\text{P/R}}$ L/M

79

1. Which one of the following could be an accurate list of the safety ratings assigned to the models, from the highest safety rating to the lowest?

   (A) Q, M, R, P, N, L
   (B) Q, R, P, L, N, M
   (C) R, P, L, N, Q, M
   (D) Q, P, R, N, M, L
   (E) L, Q, R, N, P, M

Only C remains, so the correct answer is C. Items of this kind – with answer choices consisting of complete arrangements of elements – can always be solved this way, with no more insight into the game required than a basic understanding of the rules. You don't even have to diagram the game to get an item like this one right. Even better, items such as this tend to be the first item associated with the game. Moral of the story: even if you hate a game, if the first item looks like this one you can solve it in a matter of seconds using CBT1!

Here's the second item:

2. Which one of the following must be true of N's safety rating?

   (A) It is lower than L's.
   (B) It is lower than Q's.
   (C) It is higher than L's.
   (D) It is higher than M's.
   (E) It is higher than P's

Key Strategies for Setting up Logic Games and Solving the Questions

This is a categorical "must be true" item with a reasonably focused stem – we are concerned about N's position. Scanning the answer choices, we see that they each involve placing N relative to another element. Since we have drawn consequences from the rules, and since the item has such a focused stem, MBT1 is probably the best approach here. And in fact our sequencing rule leads us directly to the correct answer:

R, P...N...M

This rule makes answer choice D true, so the correct answer is D.

Notice that this strategy – MBT1 – made sense here in large part because we were able to draw consequences from the rules by combining them at the beginning of the game. But what if these consequences had escaped our attention? What if we had tried to solve this item with the original rules?

Let's go back to the original rules, then, and try it again:

L M N P Q R

                                        Q...M
                    N   R, P
___ ___ ___ ___ ___ ___   P...M

Now MBT1 doesn't seem as reasonable an approach; none of the answer choices stands out as a likely consequence of the rules. We'll probably have to work through the answer choices at some point (MBT2), but the correct answer to item 1, answer choice D, gives us a possible arrangement of elements. Why not start with it? Here it is:

81

Mastering LSAT Logic Games

R	P	L	N	Q	M
___	___	___	___	___	___

This arrangement of elements makes answer choices B, C, and E false, and so all three can be eliminated instantly:

2. Which one of the following must be true of N's safety rating?

   (A) It is lower than L's.
   (B̶) It is lower than Q's.
   (C̶) It is higher than L's.
   (D) It is higher than M's
   (E̶) It is higher than P's

With only two answer choices remaining, MBT2 is much more efficient now. Let's make answer choice A false by switching L and Q in the previous arrangement:

R	P	Q	N	L	M
___	___	___	___	___	___

We have now eliminated all four incorrect answer choices, so the correct answer must be D. Even if one misses important consequences of the rules, efficient use of MBT2 and MBT3 can still lead to a solution relatively quickly.

Next item:

3. If L receives the lowest safety rating, then how many different assignments of safety ratings to models are possible?

(A) two
(B) three
(C) four
(D) five
(E) six

This is a conditional possible arrangements item. Place L in position 6:

L M N P Q R

R, P...N...M

Q...

| P/R | — | N | — | L | L/M |

Since four elements are before M, M must be in position 5:

| P/R | — | N | M | L | L/M |

Mastering LSAT Logic Games

This leaves the R-P pair and Q left to be placed, and there are only two ways to place them:

```
Q    R    P
R    P    Q    N    M    L
―    ―    ―    ―    ―    ―
P/R                     L/M
```

Thus, when L is in position 6, there are only two possible arrangements of elements. The correct answer is A.

Here's the next item:

4. Which one of the following must be false?

(A) L receives a lower safety rating than M.

(B) M receives a lower safety rating than L.

(C) N receives a lower safety rating than Q.

(D) P receives a lower safety rating than L.

(E) P receives a lower safety rating than N

This is a categorical "must be false" item, a member of the "could be true" family, with an unfocused stem. Again, with an unfocused stem there is very little guidance concerning which aspects of the rules to attend to, so CBT1 may not be especially promising here.

One tactic is to prioritize answer choices based on the elements they mention. For instance, answer choices C and E both mention N, an element whose placement is determined by the rules. With so much known about N, it is more likely that any violation of the rules committed by one of these answer choices would be relatively easy to spot, and so one might attend to them

Key Strategies for Setting up Logic Games and Solving the Questions

first. General rule of thumb: for "must be ..." items, focus on elements you know a lot about; for "could be..." items focus on elements you know little about.

But with so many arrangements of elements at our disposal, CBT3 isn't a bad way to go, either. We have this arrangement from the previous item:

R	P	Q	N	M	L
—	—	—	—	—	—

This makes answer choices A and C true, so they can be eliminated. We then have this arrangement from item 1:

R	P	L	N	Q	M
—	—	—	—	—	—

This arrangement makes answer choice B true; eliminate B:

4. Which one of the following must be false?

   (A̶) L receives a lower safety rating than M.
   (B̶) M receives a lower safety rating than L.
   (C̶) N receives a lower safety rating than Q.
   (D) P receives a lower safety rating than L.
   (E) P receives a lower safety rating than N

With only two answer choices remaining, it is probably clear that answer choice E violates our derived sequencing rule, and so must be false. But perhaps not - let's plug in one of the remaining answer choices; how about D. Working with the arrangement above, move L to position 1, and slide the R-P pair down one position:

85

Mastering LSAT Logic Games

<u>L</u> <u>R</u> <u>P</u> <u>N</u> <u>Q</u> <u>M</u>

This arrangement makes answer choice D true, so eliminate D. The correct answer is E.

Let's look at one more item from this game:

5. L cannot be the model receiving the

   (A) highest safety rating.

   (B) second highest safety rating.

   (C) third highest safety rating.

   (D) fifth highest safety rating.

   (E) lowest safety rating.

This is a categorical "must be false" item, but with a focused stem. This stem tells us precisely which aspects of the rules to attend to – positions that L cannot occupy, and so the item is a good candidate for CBT1. Our diagram suggests a couple of candidates – positions 2 and 4:

```
                 [N]
___  ___  ___  ___  ___  ___
     [P/R]            L/M
```

Not surprisingly, the correct answer refers to one of these positions. The correct answer is B.

These items illustrate nicely how a single item admits of a variety of reasonable approaches to solving it. If you happen to have insight into the rules of a game or the stem of an item, it is likely that working with the rules and stem information will be the focus of your effort. Otherwise,

Key Strategies for Setting up Logic Games and Solving the Questions

one can always solve an item by working through the answer choices, a strategy that becomes much more efficient when it is paired with the use of existing arrangements of elements to show that answer choices either could be true, or else could be false, depending on the item type.

Let's try another game:

> Three members of a theater company-Gina, Henry, Inez- will perform
> A total of six tasks-booking, editing, lighting, marketing, ticketing,
> writing-on three consecutive days. Each member works on exactly
> one of the three days, and no two members work on the same
> day. Each member performs at least one task, each task is
> completed on the day on which it is begun, and is performed on no
> other day. The three-day work schedule for the members must
> satisfy the following conditions:
>> At most three tasks are performed on the same day.
>> Gina and Henry do not work on consecutive days.
>> Ticketing is performed on the third day.
>> Editing is performed after writing.
>> Booking and marketing are performed by the same member.

The stimulus introduces two sets of elements, G, H, and I; and B, E, L, M, T, and W. Both sets of elements are ordered, and the first set serves as names of groups of the second; a classic sequencing groups and elements game, in which the members of the first category serve as names for groups of elements from the second. The diagram can be a standard grouping diagram, with the group names in the top row and ordinary elements in the bottom row.

Mastering LSAT Logic Games

The scenario and first rule establish some basic constraints on the groups, which we add to the diagram. The rest of the rules are standard ordering and grouping fare:

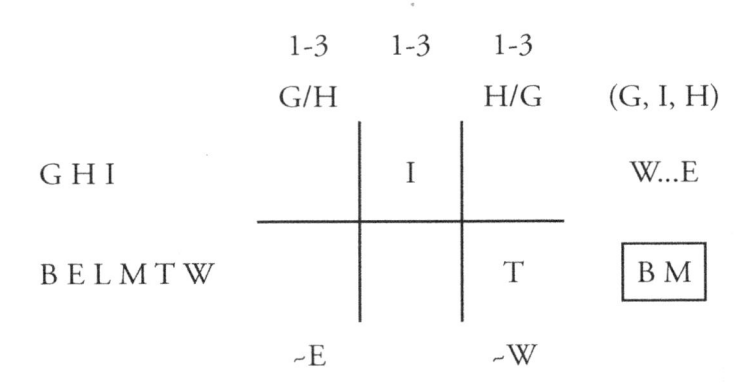

```
                1-3      1-3      1-3
                G/H      H/G     (G, I, H)
                 |        |
     G H I       |   I    |       W...E
            ─────┼────────┼─────
     B E L M T W |        |  T    | B M |
                 |        |
                ~E       ~W
```

Rule 2 can be written in a clever way: it says, in effect, that G and H are at the ends, and I is in the middle. We'll add this to the diagram as well. The other obvious consequences involve the order of E and W, which we also add to the diagram.

Notice that there are only two ways to arrange the elements on the top row, and the group size limit of three places significant constraints on allowable arrangements of elements on the bottom row as well. As a result, we should be able to draw helpful consequences from any stem conditions in the items.

Here's the first item of this game:

1. If writing and lighting are performed by the same member, then which one of the following must be false?

    (A) Henry performs editing.

    (B) Inez performs writing.

    (C) Gina performs booking.

88

Key Strategies for Setting up Logic Games and Solving the Questions

    (D)   The same member performs both booking and writing.

    (E)   The same member performs both editing and ticketing.

This is a conditional "must be false" item, a member of the "could be true" family. Let's add the stem condition to the rules, and see what follows.

There is a clear sequencing consequence – because L and W are in the same group and W is before E, L goes before E as well.

There are also a couple of grouping consequences. Because the maximum group size is three elements, neither B nor M can be in the same group with either L or W; otherwise this group would have four elements. Let's add these to our diagram:

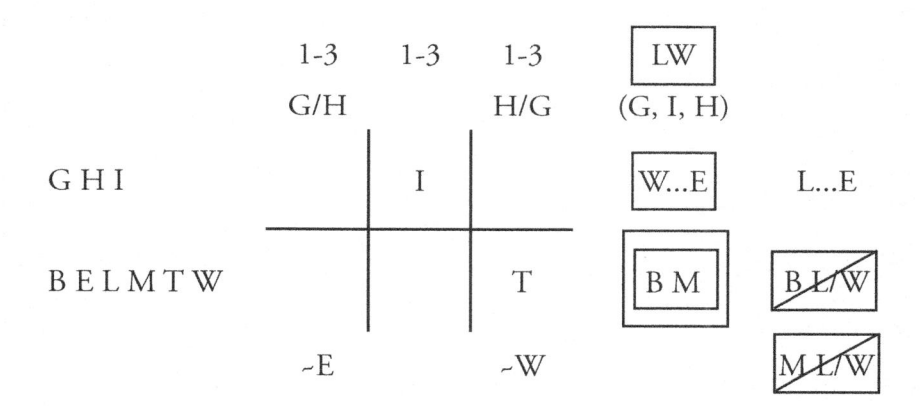

```
                1-3      1-3      1-3     | LW |
                G/H      H/G    (G, I, H)
                                          |W...E|    L...E
    G H I        |        I        |
                 |                 |
                 |                 |      | B M |   |B̶L̶/W|
    B E L M T W  |        T        |
                                          |M̶L̶/W̶|
                ~E       ~W
```

Under the circumstances, CBT1 is a good bet – just check the answer choices against these consequences. Answer choice D places B and W in the same group, and so breaks the rules. The correct answer is D.

89

But perhaps one misses these consequences. Then a combination of CBT2 and CBT3 should work. Let's try answer choice A. In order to place E in H, H must occupy position 3, with E and T. Then the other pairs must go in positions 1 and 2, in one order or the other:

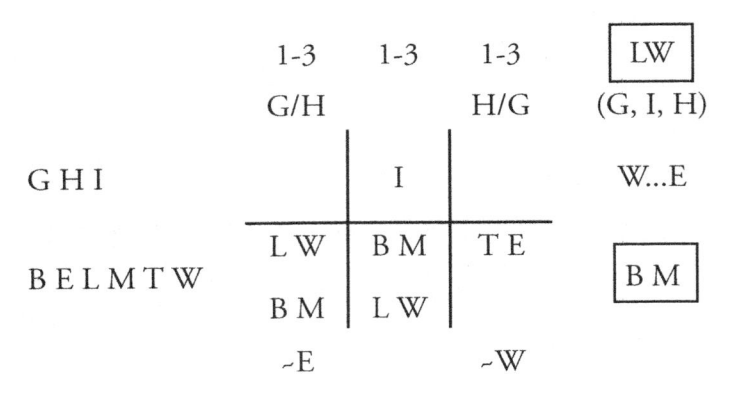

```
                  1-3     1-3     1-3      LW
                  G/H             H/G     (G, I, H)
        G H I              I              W...E
                  ─────────────────────
                  L W    B M    T E
        BELMTW                             BM
                  B M    L W
                  ~E              ~W
```

These two arrangements make answer choice A true, as well as B, C, and E. Only D remains:

1. If writing and lighting are performed by the same member, then which one of the following must be false?

    (A) Henry performs editing.
    (B) Inez performs writing.
    (C) Gina performs booking.
    (D) The same member performs both booking and writing.
    (E) The same member performs both editing and ticketing.

The correct answer is D. For this item using CBT2 and CBT3 in combination was almost as quick and efficient as relying exclusively on CBT1.

Let's try the next item:

2. If Inez performs only writing, then which one of the following must be true?

(A) Lighting is performed before editing.

(B) Lighting is performed before marketing.

(C) Marketing is performed on the first day.

(D) Editing is performed on the second day.

(E) Lighting and ticketing are performed by the same member.

This is a conditional "must be true" item with an unfocused stem. With any luck following out the consequences of the stem condition will take us to the correct answer (MBT1).

Place W in position 2, the I-group. All the remaining elements must occupy either position 1 or position 3. By the sequencing rule, E must occupy position 3. Thus B and M go in position 1:

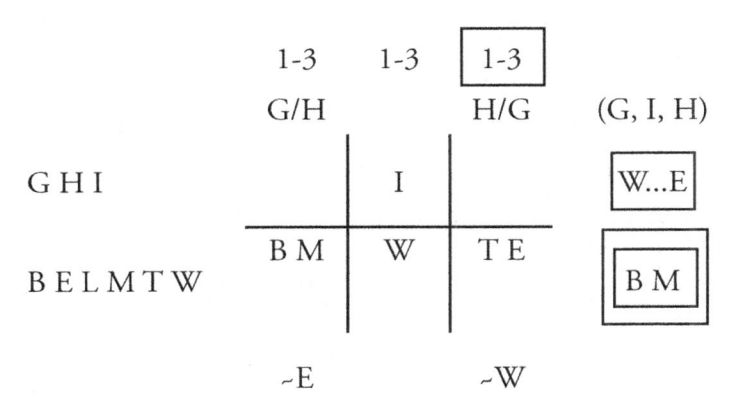

```
                    1-3      1-3     1-3
                    G/H      H/G    (G, I, H)

        G H I                 I     W...E
                    ─────┼─────┼─────
                    B M    W    T E
        BELMTW                        B M

                    ~E         ~W
```

Our diagram makes answer choice C true, so the correct answer is C.

91

Next item:

3. If Henry performs editing, then each of the following could be true EXCEPT

   (A) Gina performs booking.

   (B) Gina performs writing.

   (C) Henry performs lighting.

   (D) Henry performs marketing.

   (E) Inez performs writing.

This is another conditional "must be false" item, as was the first item. We'll follow out the consequences of the stem, then check the answer choices to see if one of them violates the rules.

Let's place E with H. As we saw above, this requires that they occupy position 3 with T, and so G is in position 1. Thus B and M together must occupy either position 1 or position 2:

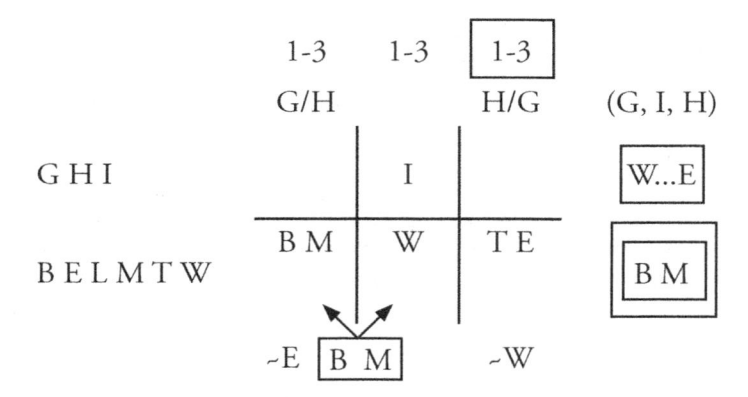

```
                1-3      1-3     1-3
                G/H      H/G            (G, I, H)
  G H I                   I             W...E
                ─────┼─────┼─────
                 B M │  W  │ T E
  B E L M T W                            B M
                     ↖ ↗
                 ~E  B M   ~W
```

Answer choice D places M in H, but this requires that four elements be in this group, which violates the rules. Since answer choice D must be false, the correct answer is D.

Key Strategies for Setting up Logic Games and Solving the Questions

Alternatively, filling in our diagram and seeing which answer choices it makes true – CBT3 – isn't a bad way to finish. Here's one placement of elements:

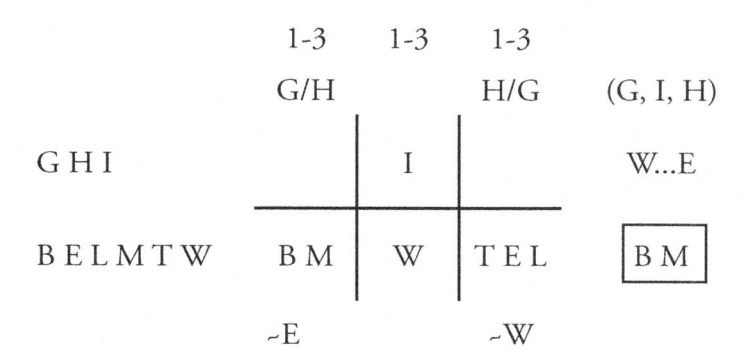

```
                    1-3      1-3      1-3
                    G/H              H/G      (G, I, H)
          G H I              I                 W...E
                    ─────┼────────┼──────
       B E L M T W   B M  │   W    │ T E L    │ B M │
                    ~E               ~W
```

This arrangement of elements makes answer choices A, C, and E true, and so eliminates three of the four incorrect answer choices in one swoop.

On to the next item:

4. If booking and editing are performed on the same day, then how many different work schedules are possible?

   (A) two
   (B) three
   (C) four
   (D) five
   (E) six

93

This is a conditional arrangement of elements item. Let's place E with B. But by rule 5 this means E, B, and M form one group alone. But E cannot occupy position 1, and T is already in position 3, so these three elements are in position 2 with I:

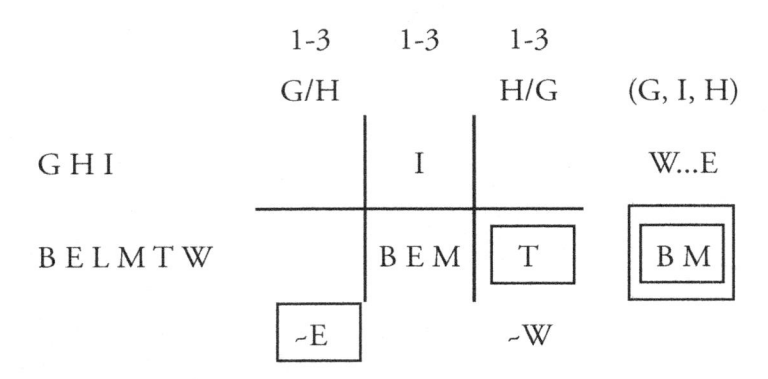

	1-3 G/H	1-3 H/G	(G, I, H)
G H I		I		W...E
B E L M T W		B E M	T	B M
	~E	~W	

We have two elements left to place, L and W. W cannot occupy position 3 and position 2 is full, so W is in position 1. L, then, can occupy either position 1 or position 3, so there are only two possible arrangements of elements in the bottom row:

	1-3 G/H	1-3 H/G	(G, I, H)
G H I		I		W...E
B E L M T W	W L	B E M	T L	B M
	~E		~W	

These two possibilities, times the two possible placements of G and H in the top row, result in four total possible arrangements total. The correct answer is C.

Key Strategies for Setting up Logic Games and Solving the Questions

The next item introduces a slight complication – it changes the rules of the game by suspending one rule and replacing it with another. This is an extremely rare item type, found only once every several tests and always the last item of an item set. Take a look:

5. Suppose the condition that Gina and Henry do not work on consecutive days is replaced with the condition that Gina works on the day immediately before the day Henry works. If all other conditions remain the same, and if Inez performs marketing but not writing, which one of the following must be true?

   (A) Gina performs lighting.
   (B) Henry performs editing.
   (C) Henry performs ticketing.
   (D) Inez performs lighting.
   (E) Inez performs ticketing.

To begin with, the new rule requires significant changes to the diagram: G can't be last, H can't be first, and I must be on one end or the other:

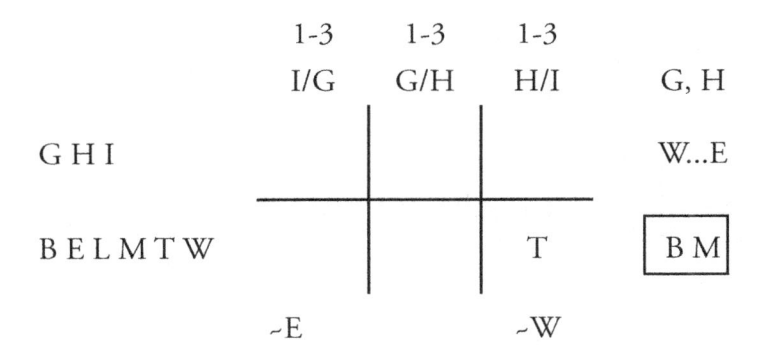

```
              1-3     1-3     1-3
              I/G     G/H     H/I        G, H

    G H I                                 W...E

    B E L M T W             T            | B M |

              ~E              ~W
```

The stem conditions are difficult since there is not a unique way to implement them: B and M are with I, but this could be either in position 1 or in position 3. And the placement of W depends on the placement of I.

95

Mastering LSAT Logic Games

In this case, even though we have a conditional stem, we may be better off just listing a few arrangements of elements and trying to eliminate, a version of MBT3. Let's consider both placements of I, B, and M in the diagram.

If I is in position 1, then by the stem condition W and E must be in positions 2 and 3, with G and H, respectively. L can then occupy any position:

```
                1-3     1-3     1-3
                G/I     G/H     H/I      G, H
    G H I        I   |   G   |   H      W...E
               ─────┼───────┼─────
    B E L M T W  B M |   W   |  T E     │B M│
                -E           -W
```

This arrangement of elements allows answer choices A, D, and E to be false, so eliminate A, D, and E. Now let's move I, B, and M to position 3, and draw the consequences:

```
                1-3     1-3     1-3
                G/I     G/H     H/I      G, H
    G H I        G   |   H   |   I      W...E
               ─────┼───────┼─────
    B E L M T W  W   |   E   | T B M    │B M│
                -E           -W
```

This arrangement makes answer choice C false, so eliminate C.

5. Suppose the condition that Gina and Henry do not work on consecutive days is replaced with the condition that Gina works on the day immediately before the day Henry works. If all other conditions remain the same, and if Inez performs marketing but not writing, which one of the following must be true?

(A) Gina performs lighting.
(B) Henry performs editing.
(C) Henry performs ticketing.
(D) Inez performs lighting.
(E) Inez performs ticketing.

The only remaining answer choice is B, so B is correct.

Conclusion

This last couple of games illustrates two important points. First, it is a mistake to think that there is a "best way" to approach any particular item. What works best for one test taker may not for another; indeed, what works well for you today may not work as well tomorrow. Insight into the rules, attention span, level of interest, etc. all contribute to whether you will be more successful with one approach than another.

Second, although the strategies can be thought of as distinct approaches to solving items, in practice successful test takers blend them into an integrated approach. One might focus on the rules first before working through answer choices, for instance; or one might borrow an arrangement of elements used to evaluate one answer choice in order to help evaluate the others. Flexibility is the key to solving items quickly and efficiently.

You now have all the tools necessary to master the AR section of the LSAT. The next step is to become as familiar as possible with the games and items likely to appear on your LSAT. The best way to do this, of course, is to practice with real games from past LSAT tests. Find the complete selection of official LSAT PrepTests at LSAC.org.

We wish you good luck on the LSAT, in law school, and in your future legal career!

Key Strategies for Setting up Logic Games and Solving the Questions

FREE
EASY LSAT CHEAT SHEET!

Get instant access to the free Easy LSAT Cheat Sheet I've created for you at **LSATUnplugged.com**.

Made in the USA
Las Vegas, NV
15 August 2024